G. Ferguson

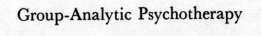

Group-Analytic Psychotherapy

Group-Analytic Psychotherapy
Method and Principles

S. H. FOULKES

MARESFIELD LIBRARY
LONDON

First published by Gordon & Breach, Science Publishers Ltd, 1975
Reprinted 1986
    by H. Karnac (Books) Ltd.,
    58 Gloucester Road,
    London S.W.7

Second Impression 1991

Distributed in the U.S.A. by
Brunner/Mazel, Inc.,
19, Union Square West,
New York, NY 10003.

Printed by BPCC Wheatons Ltd, Exeter
ISBN 0 946439 22 2

To Elizabeth Foulkes

Acknowledgements

In giving examples, I have used material based on my experience and notes taken while at the Bethlem Royal Hospital and the Maudsley Hospital and while Visiting Professor at the Department of Psychiatry, University of North Carolina, Chapel Hill. I wish here to thank these two institutions for the facilities extended to me.

I wish also to express my thanks to Dr Vivienne Cohen who at an early stage in the writing of this book assisted me in some of the formulations which I have used chiefly in Chapter V. I also acknowledge the use I have made of notes by Harold Kaye when he was co-conductor in one of my groups, and take this opportunity of thanking him.

Last but not least, I would like to thank my personal secretary, Elizabeth Gromyko, for her most competent and loyal assistance.

S. H. F.

Contents

Introduction

This decade has been called the decade of the group. All kinds of groups have been formed by all types of individuals. Groups are supposed to be the new panacea and are intended to relieve everything from loneliness to sexual impotency. Most of the groups are quasi-religious and the results are largely testimonial in nature. For those who want to gain some systematic awareness and insight into the practice and theory of a professionally led group, S. H. Foulkes has presented a detailed and practical approach to his work with groups.

Foulkes has been a practising psychoanalyst for almost half a century and has worked with groups for over thirty years. He is a highly trained psychiatrist and psychoanalyst whom I am privileged to call a colleague and friend. This book, to be followed by a companion volume on theory, captures the flavor and spirit of the highly trained and experienced practitioner as he goes about the task of organizing and conducting a group. The book also captures the warmth and humanity of a professional who is deeply devoted to his patients, his profession and humanity at large.

This work is an original. It stems from the author's own practice and approach to his patients in a variety of settings, ranging from the military to the mental hospital to the large general hospital as well as patients in private practice. Thus the reader is able to capture the entire spectrum of clinical practice. Foulkes also manages to share his nuggets of wisdom which are the distillation of many years of clinical practice. These "gems" are valuable for both the student and experienced practitioner who wants to sample another point of view.

What is particularly helpful to those of us on the USA side of the Atlantic is to find out how our British colleagues began to work with groups and the approaches they devised, relatively free from American influences. Foulkes has presented his way of working with patients, how he goes about selecting them and what his final goals are. He is completely dedicated to his task and yet he has maintained an overall vision of what the task is to be in terms of relatedness to the larger society and culture. Even his convictions, some of which I would be in marked disagreement with, are presented with a refreshing candor and no apologies. He does not engage in gobbledy-gook and profess to be all things to all people. This is what he believes and this is how he goes about doing his job — as he perceives his task. Nowhere does he profess to be a new messiah or claim to relieve the pain and suffering of all mankind.

Every author has his own way of presenting material. I would recommend to the reader especially, Chapter VII — the conductor (therapist) as a person and his training. This chapter captures the profundity of Foulkes' approach to what makes a therapist in a rather pithy fashion. This statement by Foulkes is particularly important when one observes that groups are being led by every conceivable type of group leader with every conceivable type of personal problem. Foulkes "tells it like it is" and "lets the chips fall where they may". I know him to be a gentleman and not a person who invites or promotes controversy, but in a dignified and succinct fashion, he sets forth the qualities that make for a group therapist. I would recommend reading this chapter first so that the reader begins to feel the humanity of the author. Perhaps this is unfair to the logical sequence of Foulkes' presentation — but I thought I would set down my personal preference.

When one observes the plethora of techniques and gimmicks that have been presented to students of group therapy, Foulkes' work is a breath of fresh air. Some of his statements will surely stimulate students to study further and look for new ideas in approaching work with groups. This is what good books should do. S. H. Foulkes has done this. Enjoy the book.

Foulkes has informed me that he always aimed to build up the foundations of a comprehensive and really adequate and specific theory for group analysis. I look forward to his companion book on theory.

MAX ROSENBAUM

SECTION I

GROUP-ANALYTIC ORIENTATION

CHAPTER 1

What Is Group-Analytic Psychotherapy ?

Group-analytic psychotherapy is a method of group psychotherapy initiated by myself from 1940 onwards in private psychiatric practice and out-patient clinics. It grew out of and is inspired by my experiences as a psychoanalyst, but it is *not* a psychoanalysis of individuals in a group. Nor is it the psychological treatment of a group by a psychoanalyst. It is a form of psychotherapy *by* the group, *of* the group, including its conductor. Hence the name: group-analytic psychotherapy.

The therapist-analyst helps in this process and puts his expert knowledge and his education as a person at the service of the group. He is the responsible administrator, a task he should fulfil in a flexible, dynamic, creative way; his personality and method are the most important individual factors in this procedure. Yet he leads the group only exceptionally and has therefore been called the conductor, the guardian and guide, of the group-analytic group.

No such form of group psychotherapy existed at the time, neither in this country nor on the continent of Europe, or elsewhere, including the U.S.A., as postwar acquaintance proved. In the U.S.A., approaches had been made to groups and classes of sick persons. Also in the States, the mutual analysis of a group of psychiatrists under the inspiration of Trigant Burrow, going back to the twenties, had at that time stimulated the present writer. The only two analysts who to my knowledge had begun to practise a psychoanalytical approach to groups at the same time, or perhaps a year or two earlier, were Louis Wender and Paul Schilder; but their practice was nothing like my own, even in its very early stages.

Group-analytic psychotherapy has not only been consistently developing and expanding to the present day, but its characteristics, its principles in practice and theory, and even many of its terms have been taken over — sometimes acknowledged, for the most part anonymously — into the current literature and into more or less new types of approaches in this still rapidly expanding field.

This account confines itself to group-analytic psychotherapy, or for short and in a slightly more comprehensive meaning group analysis, but it can serve as a useful model for all forms of deep-going group psychotherapy, insofar as they are concerned not merely with helping to alleviate suffering by ventilation and understanding, with liberating the individual from excessive social and sexual and, alas, aggressive inhibitions, but in addition with uncovering unconscious conflicts and paving the way for their resolution, and based therefore ultimately on verbal forms of communication and not on acting.

The most interesting part of this work is perhaps the theoretical foundations on which it rests and which it has in turn developed. These are part of a total revolution in psychiatry, psychotherapy and even slowly affecting psychoanalysis, reflecting the rapid change of interpersonal development in the world at large. A separate volume will be devoted to these new theoretical and clinical concepts. Here we shall only be concerned with method and practice. The subject moreover will be treated somewhat personally, insofar as it will be confined to my own experience as a clinician, teacher, supervisor. The account may in addition appear a little uneven or unbalanced. What is well-known today (albeit not well enough), although it may be basic, will be treated briefly. Relatively more space will be given to methodological features which are less well-known or as yet unpublished. Altogether this is meant to be a practical handbook rather than a comprehensive text, with sufficient illustrations for immediate use.

As will be seen, the principles developed and maintained in their pure form in the standard types of the therapeutic *group-analytic group* can be applied to all forms of human groups even if they are not primarily therapeutic, but are closer to a process of living-learning and of comprehensive problem solving. It is important to note that, whereas the general principles remain valid, the parameters of each situation can be precisely defined, so as to determine clearly the application of these principles to the particular task and situation in hand.

GENERAL PRINCIPLES

What are these principles in their *general* form?

1) The total situation is the frame of reference for all operations and for the interpretation (understanding) of all observable events. *Situation* in this connection comprises all the objective reality circumstances and the rules, explicit or implicit, observed in the encounter.

2) All persons involved in the enterprise, institution or project, be they directors, managers, technicians, workmen or customers in industry, administrators, teachers or students in universities, doctors, nursing staff, patients or relatives in the case of a hospital and so forth must be brought together and meet regularly for full and frank discussion and interchange of information and viewpoints. This has to be supplemented by free discussions in smaller groups selected in the light of their special part functions, as well as in *ad hoc* groups spontaneously arising from particular circumstances. Maximal mutual awareness and communication is the aim, shared as far as possible by all concerned and therefore enabling the whole group to take an active part in their enterprise. Given good leadership such an objective is realistic as we showed experimentally at Northfield Military Neurosis Centre during World War II. The day will come when whole communities and nations will deal with their affairs in this way.

3) The leader, or team of leaders — in the case of the therapeutic group the conductor — is perhaps the most important variable determining the prevailing culture and tradition of the group. He must in turn use his ability in the best interest of the group, he is its first servant. He must follow the group, guiding it to its legitimate goal and help it to cope with destructive and self-destructive elements, ideally making them unnecessary. It is of the utmost importance for the leader's function that he recognises and keeps within the dynamic boundaries of the situation, that he knows and respects what can and what cannot be done or said in the circumstances from which his own mandate is derived and defined.

4) It is essential that the situation is not taken on the basis of appearances according to the expectation ordinarily connected with it, but that covert reactions should be brought into the open, that is to say the situation should be explored not as what it *appears* to be, but as what it *really* is.

DIFFERENT TYPES OF GROUP IN OPERATION

The general principles outlined above are applicable to all human groups. Their application must *follow* the differing conditions dynamically. The situations in which a group-analytic approach can be practised more particularly fall into two basic categories:

a) *The operative group, or life group* — that is to say the group in which the problems or conflicts actually arise.

b) *Groups of unconnected individuals formed for special purposes* Such groups can be large or small, and change their character according to the problems under consideration. They are on a continuum from therapeutic to learning processes. In this context we shall mostly concentrate on therapy in our examples.

We shall now illustrate by way of a few brief examples, selected from my own experience, how these principles operate in the different types of groups, and work our way up, so to speak, to the group-analytic group in its various modifications. The reader will notice that one of the most important variables is the way in which unconscious processes, always important, are handled on a scale from mere observation and consideration to full exploration as charac-teristic of the group-analytic group.

For more detail and theory I must refer to my various writings and books.† A book on the most important theoretical foundations and concepts is in preparation.

a)   1) *Large Groups and Institutions*

Example: *The Northfield Therapeutic Community*

Today the concept of a hospital as a *therapeutic community* is widely accepted and practised. It was first established experimentally during World War II at Northfield Military Neurosis Centre, near Birmingham. Encouraged and supported by the late J. R. Rees, then Director of Army Psychiatry, and especially also Ronald Hargreaves, a team of us, consisting of Tom Main, Harold Bridger, myself, and for a while Joshua Bierer, set to work transforming the culture of the Hospital and its Training Wing, training and educating the staff, or most of them, in a new approach to our psychotherapeutic and rehabilitation task. Many influences and various experiences which had shaped us came together, were exchanged and reintegrated. I myself had been at Northfield quite some time before the others arrived and had introduced group psychotherapy in my own ward, as did Joshua Bierer in his own style some time later. What may be less well-known, by the way, is that I there made novel use of psychoanalytical principles in individual psychotherapy. For both

†*Introduction to Group-Analytic Psychotherapy*, London, Heinemann, (1948).
Group Psychotherapy, Harmondsworth, Penguin Books, (1957). Revised Editions (1965, 1973). Jointly with E. J. Anthony.
Therapeutic Group Analysis, London, Allen and Unwin, (1964).

types of therapy I had been well prepared by my wartime civilian experiences. From my point of view the *Northfield Experiment* was an extension of the principles discussed above, which were in part first developed as this opportunity arose. More detailed accounts of this work is contained in *Introduction to Group-Analytic Psychotherapy* and in *Therapeutic Group Analysis.* Some reports of our work, by various authors, were published in the *Bulletin of the Menninger Clinic,* Volume 10, May 1946. This resulted from a two-day visit by leading American psychiatrists who were very favourably impressed by our new methods and their results. They told us that there was no equivalent of this in the U.S.A. Many famous visitors from this country as well as from abroad expressed themselves in the same sense.

Gradually, the whole hospital became a coherent, but not an "organised" body, a community insofar as there was a free flow of communication between the patients themselves, the staff and between patients and staff. "Free" as far as was commensurate with the many different occasions of contact and co-operation. Ward meetings, social evenings, group activities, more specific treatment groups or individual psychotherapy, staff meetings, doctors' conferences, etc. were all seen as part of a coherent process. The interrelationship between all these different occasions and their interdependence became clear. Treatment was understood to begin with the soldiers' arrival, if not before, and contact allowing for follow-up of the results was maintained with the patients' own military units long after discharge from the hospital. Changes as to symptoms, behaviour and attitude, sometimes quite considerable, were thus subjected to the best of all tests, the test of life, as reported by independent witnesses, who knew nothing of each other and who were certainly not biased in the psychiatrists' favour. The same was true inside the hospital itself. The patients were active, responsible participants in their "cure". They were given the greatest possible freedom of choice as to what they wished to do, how they wished to spend their time in the Hospital. With a very few possible exceptions they did not abuse the quite unusual liberty to express their feelings, thoughts, worries, anxieties, criticisms or rebellious anger with complete frankness and without fear of retaliation. Doctors, nursing staff and patients became aware, in living reality, that and how they were interlocking in their reactions to a shared context of problems.

This is a sketchy account of an experience which occupied me, for one, day and night for about three years. I hope it will serve as an illustration of principles, which have since proved their value in psychiatric and other hospitals, as well as in prisons, industry and in institutions of all sorts, especially also educational ones. Of still greater importance are the methods and principles, as they grew from the far more subtle observations in the small groups, based ultimately on group psychotherapy inspired by the psychoanalytical approach. It is not too much to say that these new methods and principles increasingly transform the whole of social life, at least in the West.

2) Small Groups

All these groups, whether large or small, forming an inherent part of the large group or community or institution in question, have certain features in common which differentiate them sharply from the analytical psychotherapeutic group proper, which will be in the centre of this book. The members of these groups know each other and meet in ordinary life, though their meetings and contacts are on the whole confined to more or less organised common activities. These may concern their work, common interests in literature, science, philosophy, their religion, politics, or recreation, be it music, dancing or sport. If they function and perform together as a group, as a "team", the improved function of the whole group is the task. Thus the group itself becomes the foreground (figure), and the individuals are seen as background. Fortunately, one cannot separate groups and the individuals composing them, except by artificial abstraction, and as the group improves, the individuals benefit also.

More often, however, such groups are formed from individuals with separate interests. All they have in common is for instance that they work in the same factory, or in the same department of a larger institution. For the rest they may be competitors, mistrust each other, be curious or otherwise hostile; or the members of such a group may perform similar duties, as for example managers working apart from each other.

The principle is therefore that of a "free discussion" of their shared problems. They should be frank in this, participate actively and deal with unnecessary frictions and negative emotions. Certain features of psychotherapy enter into this and the participants may overcome their own conflicts, gain in liberty and grow mentally. It is important however not to conduct such a group as if it were a psychotherapeutic group. The boundaries are *limited* and it is not desirable and could even be damaging to introduce confidential matters from their sexual or family life.

A particular type of such a group, the supervisory seminar which I conducted over many years with my registrars at the Maudsley Hospital will be described in Section III when we come to deal with the therapist-conductor and his training. Provided we respect the limitations imposed by the situation and the particular circumstances, these types of group are nevertheless psychotherapeutic groups. They can be seen either at their place of work or in a setting specially reserved for the purpose.

Example: *A Chaplain's group*

I owe this observation to Professor David R. Hawkins now at the University of Virginia, but at that time at another North American university when, during the time I was there as Visiting Professor, he discussed the group with me. Some years later he gave a most interesting paper on his observations to the Group-Analytical Society (London). Since he has not yet published the material himself, I shall here pick out a few of the salient points particularly in respect of method.

This is a prototype of a group which was already in existence and was seen with a view of providing therapy for the group *as a group*. The members were university chaplains or ministers of various denominations who worked with the students at this American University. The group enabled the therapist also to gain insight into the particular features which seemed characteristic for the profession itself. An important part of the chaplains' duties was student counselling. They were thus in a sense students of this group method for their own purposes.

Dr Hawkins gives a most interesting account of the development of this group and makes many important observations. About the technique he says:

> In retrospect I was too attacking in my interpretations. They were correct, but too deep-going and too direct at this point in the group's history. This was related to counter-transference issues.

It might be mentioned that amongst the counter-transference influences entered personal relationships with different group members on the part of the therapist, (with one he was close friends, etc.) which in this situation could not be avoided, but presents particular difficulties. Apparently in spite of these complications, the group was very successful and undoubtedly improved its own and its members' function. The special situation relating to the constant contact between the members and sometimes even with the therapist outside the group sessions was clearly faced. The conclusion drawn was to keep a middle line between treating the group on a merely supportive level or going into intensive insight therapy. The therapist himself constantly maintained an analytic attitude. He operated analytically but restricted the breadth of the analysis. To quote Professor Hawkins: "... there was therapy in depth, but in a special sector ..." It was proposed to term such an approach as "focussed" or "sector group analysis".

Here is Professor Hawkins' own summary:

1) A group of university chaplains who met regularly once a week asked to be and were given group psychotherapy for two years.

2) 12 out of 13 members participated the first year. 8 out of 11 participated the second year.

3) A major focus of the therapy was improvement of the total group function.

4) A modified form of the analytic approach was used. Certain areas were proscribed. In certain sectors there was therapy in depth. This approach might be termed "focussed, sector-group analysis".

5) Observations were made on the interrelationships between personality dynamics and societal role as it affected the group function.

This group experience is a good example of an operating group, in this case treated mainly as a group and in view of its function as a group.

CHAPTER 2

The Treatment of the Life Group

NETWORK, PLEXUS

We are here concerned with problems as they arise in an interconnected, existing network in life. By contrast with the previous chapter, these people are very closely and intimately connected and their interactional network concerns the central area of their lives.

The family itself is the prototype of such a group, but I have stressed from the beginning that in psychological terms such a network includes persons who are not in the ordinary sense of the term family members.

Originally I used the term *network* and also *nexus*. Both these terms have since been used widely and with different meanings, so that I propose to use a special name for this concept of the intimate dynamic network with which we are concerned, and to call it *complexus* or for short *plexus*. (What is meant by that is that a relatively small number of people, who include the family, group themselves dynamically as the process of treatment proceeds, group themselves round the central person — the patient — especially in connection with his conflicts which are significant for the disturbance for which he has come to consult us.)

The network at large is manifold. There are in our culture always quite a number of such networks to which each individual belongs. How these groups relate to each other, and how any individual relates his membership of these different groups to each other or, respectively does not relate them, is highly characteristic.

From the point of view of *method* it is at this stage important for us to note that we do not construct or anticipate such a complexus of people and call them together for treatment. What happens is that we build up from what may be called the central patient, we then follow the psychodynamics as we become aware of them to a group of people around him, who turn out to have an essential connection with his basic conflict, symptoms and problems. The basis of the method is very much like that employed in group-analytic family therapy, the members of the plexus are seen in various constellations as the psychodynamic progress of the treatment commands. The great importance of such an approach lies in the theoretical consequences it has for our view of psychopathology and of the social nature of mental processes about which I will speak later.

The term *network* was used to express the fact that our individual patient is, in essence, merely a symptom of a disturbance of equilibrium in the intimate network of which he is a part. Personally, I used the term *network* deliberately in analogy to my teacher in the mid-twenties, the neuro-biologist Kurt Goldstein, then in Frankfurt. He was a pioneer of the view that the nervous system can best be understood in theory and practice not as a complicated sum of individual neurons but that on the contrary it reacts consistently as a whole. He called this a network and called the individual neuron cell a *nodal point*. For this reason I called the total system of persons who belong together in their reaction a network, and the *individuals* composing it correspond to *nodal points*. It fits well that this network in its most intimate part should be called *plexus*. Such a view leads to a new orientation in psychopathology and in psychotherapy. This belongs to the theory of group analysis and will not be dealt with here.

The practical consequences are considerable and will occupy us here. In studying such networks systematically I could demonstrate clinically, in quite unselected patients who came for treatment, that every single one had such a *plexus* around him, or was part of such a *complexus*. In practice, and this is the most important point methodologically, it does not amount to more than a handful of people, if one calls into the area of treatment only those who have a direct significance for the patient's conflicts and their possible solution or who stand in the way of any such solution.

FAMILY TREATMENT AND DIAGNOSIS

There is nothing like a family to cause you mental instability. (Physiotherapist, anonymous).

This is today perhaps the most widespread and common mode of group treatment and has been cultivated in a great number of varities. This was not the case when, in 1940, I first came across this as a treatment proposition, or rather, it came to me. I have published a few examples of that period.

As a psychoanalyst one was aware of the fact that each patient is closely interlinked and interacting with those who are nearest to him or her. But as a psychoanalyst one would strictly abstain not only from treating members of the patient's family at the same time but even from seeing them at all, if possible. This makes good sense in the psychoanalytic method which seeks to refer the problems back entirely to their inner meaning for the isolated individual patient. This has to do with the development and handling of the transference situation which becomes decisively changed as soon as the therapist becomes mixed up with others than the one person under treatment. Thus it was a very essential step for me to accept the total family as a network of people and to treat them together in the same room and at the same time. It was a big step for me when I first faced this situation, though I had already been prepared for it through my experiences with groups.

The area to which the greatest attention has since been paid is in families which have produced schizophrenic members. In psychotic breakdowns, especially in schizophrenia, the interrelationship with the family both in a horizontal and vertical way is particularly easy to see. In this connection I want to mention especially the work of T. Lidz, R. D. Scott, R. D. Laing and A. Esterson and many others who have devoted much attention to this subject as well as to its theoretical consequences. As to the family treatment of neuroses, perhaps the works of J. Ehrenwald, Nathan Ackerman and Martin Grotjahn (who have all written books on the subject) are the most noteworthy. I myself have treated families only off and on, sometimes with considerable success and in a very short time, relatively speaking.

I have been especially impressed however by the examination of the family as a psychodiagnostic procedure. Such an exploration often reveals that the patient who is supposed to be the main object of treatment has only a very limited chance and scope for change. As a diagnostic procedure it seems to me to be a very important new method of approach, since it can save many years of relatively futile treatment of intensive psychoanalysis, at great monetary cost to the patient. I have introduced a number of colleagues into this approach to the family network from a group-analytic point of view, both at the Maudsley Hospital and at the Group-Analytic Society (London). Some, as for instance, Professor David Maddison in Sydney, have published their experience. At the present time, among my closer co-operators, Dr A. C. R. Skynner devotes considerable attention to this method as does Mrs Sheila Thompson from the point of view of a psychiatric social worker rather than a psychotherapist.

The essential method lies in the fact that we are ready to see the different members of the family together in various combinations, sometimes alone, with the presenting problem or problems as they arise in the centre. Personally, as I have mentioned, I accepted families for treatment when they came to me, and enlarged the number of participants in the treatment situation as the natural psychodynamic development demanded. It may of course be that the central problem is not particularly strongly located in the patient originally referred. The point not to be forgotten is that though such a family live together in the most intimate way, the fact that they meet and share the therapist together is the exceptional occasion in their life. In this respect the family group is the exact opposite of the standard group-analytic group which will be in the centre of this book. In saying that such a family is inevitably a whole group, a whole, it does not follow that we address it and treat it all the time as a whole; on the contrary, here as at any time we treat the individuals composing this group in the context of the group.

THE GROUP-ANALYTIC APPROACH TO THE FAMILY OR PLEXUS

These can be taken together as far as method is concerned in that the treatment of the family and that of the plexus, which very often includes the family, are essentially similar.

It is important to keep in mind that we cannot possibly think of treating the whole network which would include an almost infinite number of people, but only those who, as in a family have an intimate and significant share in the presenting problems, grouped round the central patient, who for our purposes is the patient who originally came to see us for treatment. It is clear that not all the members share literally all that is going on all the time, but it must be equally clear that everything that is going on between any of them, anything communicated can be shared by them with the doctor and that there are no secrets in this respect. Such a treatment does not usually take the course of a regular series of sessions, once or twice a week, but at times there will be more sessions, at times longer intervals, in a flexible manner. There may be some individuals, on the fringes as it were, whose attendance, though important, is necessary only once or twice.

The intensity of such treatment is astounding where it succeeds or where it can succeed. This has partly to do with the fact that the people are so intimately connected that they work out the stimuli received very intensively and the session itself acts mainly as a catalyst for the changes going on. In spite of having at times good successes with such treatment, it seemed clear to me that this could not work in many cases, and that it was necessary to resort to other ways of dealing with the problem as for instance individual or group-analytic treatment.

However the *psychodiagnostic* value of these meetings can hardly be overrated; while fascinating from a theoretical point of view, they are of great importance also from a point of view of practical method. *In practice,* under favourable circumstances, one can achieve solutions and considerable improvements with relatively few sessions. The handling of the transference is very different from that in the individual situation though not essentially different from our group-analytic groups; indeed it is easier in that we have to deal with a coherent organism; the interest in each other, the interdependence upon each other, being a strong natural factor, whereas by contrast in the standard group-analytic situation the opposite is the case. Obviously, the *therapist* should be *impartial,* trying to see, and to make the members of such a group see, the *motivations and mutuality* of so many reactions. He must avoid being a referee or a court of justice, he should not express valuations or give directions, just as in any other analytical type of psychotherapy.

Another practical merit of such an approach lies in the avoidance of treating the "wrong patient" or treating anybody at all when the total network group, the plexus, is in need of sanitation. Often enough there is too much resistance to make this possible. Often enough it becomes quite clear that and why closely interconnected persons cannot be frank towards each other and have secrets in their lives which they are absolutely unwilling to give up.

THE ORIGINAL NUCLEAR FAMILY

In the original, nuclear family there is a special opportunity to consider the longitudinal network in its chronological sequence, as it is passed on from parents to children, from grandparents to parents and so forth, over many generations. This very intimate interlinked system of interaction and transaction is best seen as a complex interaction of *processes* which *penetrate* the individuals composing such a network. I have therefore called these *transpersonal processes.*

In a planned book on theory, I hope to deal with what I believe to be the limitations of the so-called *inner-object theory* as against the *theory of interacting processes, and interacting unconscious communications* which I propose.

As far as I can see this primary family can best be studied at a later stage when the children are more or less adolescent or even adult. One can then get a clear picture as to the way in which they have been moulded and forced into shape by the conditions prevailing in the family into which they were born and of which they form a part. Later this influence manifests itself as transference and repetition-compulsion. These form part of the current ongoing interaction at the same time as representing the past intruding into the present. In the language of inner object theory, which has its own though limited validity, the original family has become internalised and is brought into the new life situation and, in particular, into the transference situation during analytic treatment.

To indicate what I mean by such processes and why I see them interacting in a transpersonal way, let us take a very simple example. A mother, say, may react to her child as she would have liked her own mother to treat her, or, contrary to all her conscious ideas, exactly as in her own experience her own mother or father did treat her, though at the time she was in full rebellion against that. The child in turn may react in a straightforward way to this treatment or manifest reaction formations, rebel against it, develop the opposite features, develop a strong ambivalence conflict, or may totally detach himself and become withdrawn. About all these processes we are well informed through intimate psychoanalytic study. The psychoanalyst considers these complex reactions as they look from each individual by himself. He then finds mechanisms like identification, introjection, projection, projective identification. From a group-analytic point of view these are *interactions* which can only be understood as such.

Now for another example: a father, maybe a very well adapted man, has a way of being very reserved about his inner life, making it impossible to be approached beyond a certain limit. The effect upon his wife or children brings disturbing reactions. It turns out that they cannot in turn show feelings towards the father; or they have constantly to counteract him, rebel against him. He in turn may be very dissatisfied with the behaviour, lack of success or whatever it may be of his son, say, and quite unconsciously and unwittingly contribute to the son's incapacity by treating him slightingly. Perhaps he has good reason to do so from the facts and he is convinced that he means well and is merely reacting to what he considers to be the fault of his son. Now this same father may — if one has occasion to study his individual psychopathology — have been unable to find the love and understanding of his own father and mother which he needed as a child, or he may have been brought up in such a way that any feeling or expression of emotion was curtailed. So it goes on, from generation to generation, continuously linked up through the centuries, over a really unlimited term of time. It should also be understood that these are not one-to-one reactions, father to son, mother to son, mother to daughter and so forth, but are always embedded in the total goings on in the family. In that sense no two children have the same parents, nor has anyone the same brothers or sisters as the other. Having a brother is very different from being a brother to that same brother, and so forth.

I hope this indicates sufficiently what is meant by a chronological, vertical or longitudinal network. We are wont to see this in later current families and intimate networks (complexus) as transference, as something the individual brings with him as a result of his nature and of his early constellation.

I will give just a few sketches of examples of such experiences. My examples will, for simplicity's sake, be confined to the diagnostic interviews, in one case only one single interview of a married couple. On the whole I shall leave out the way in which the children or others were concerned and only mention the salient points to illustrate the barrier to successful treatment.

In the first case there was a schizophrenic girl who, according to her psychiatrist, after many years and prolonged stays in mental hospitals, was now ready to live at home with her parents. *An interview with the parents* made clear that there was a marriage with many problems. The one thing in which both parents were really united was they could not tolerate the child at home as they found her too upsetting. In short, it became quite clear that this child had absorbed like a sponge the salient and most acute problems of the parents, and her presence in the family acted like a catalyst for trouble. In spite of very good contact with the girl it was impossible to expect any help from treating her. The attempt to treat the whole family together over these problems was refused for extraneous financial reasons which objectively were not really preventing such treatment.

In another case, contact and treatment seemed to be developing well for a few hours, but the husband consistently maintained that he needed no treatment — he was perfectly clear in his mind about his problems. It should be mentioned here that these pseudo-healthy or apparently healthy members of such a conflict situation are usually the most salient people who would have to change and also the ones who are most unlikely to change. Unless this can be achieved, the treatment is bound to fail. What shall one do, if for instance one has a case in which the husband when seen alone, declares his intimate life and interest with another woman, with whom he wants to continue a relationship or even intensify it — but at the same time does not want to disturb his marriage. What shall one do, furthermore, if this husband makes it quite clear that under no circumstances would he wish to talk about his affair in front of his wife?

I am in complete agreement here with Dr. Hans Preuss who wrote on Marital Group Therapy in *Group Analysis: International Panel and Correspondence* (GAIPAC) Vol. IV/1 making this very same point.

My next example I shall give somewhat more extensively in transcript, leaving out, however, a number of very significant factors, here, as elsewhere, for reasons of discretion. As ususal the convincing nature of the example suffers from this, but I hope it will illustrate some of the points under discussion.

PRELIMINARY INTERVIEW — MARITAL COUPLE

Dr . . . what is the trouble between you?
A . . . Mm . . .
Dr   We can talk quite frankly . . .
A   You undoubtedly know that I have been treated here very successfully . .
Dr   Yes
A   My wife . . . er . . . can I speak quite openly?
Dr   Yes, indeed . . .
A   This is purely how it strikes me. I may be quite wrong in this . . when I was first treated, when I was really ill, my wife did her very best to stand by me. She . . was . . really first class . . and as I began to get better, as I began to improve so she became depressed, anxious and so on . . and then she sought help from someone who was an analyst . . that I didn't like . . and through one thing and another an atmosphere arose which made life extremely difficult . . finally through some investigation I made . . and I asked my wife rather forcefully to tell me . . as a result of which my wife has been under some considerable strain through this . . I appreciate that . .
Dr   Yes . . tell me, what did you suspect?
A   The fact that no mention was ever made of me or my boy . . and the biggest trouble in the family has been with my eldest boy . . so far as my wife was concerned . . this was at the beginning . . then various other things happened, small . . you see . .

Dr   No mention was made in her analysis . . how do you know that?

A   Because I asked her . .

Dr   I see . . by the way, may I just ask you . . how long was that treatment, and how often . .?

Mrs A   . . Three times a week . . I started in . . at the beginning of March last year . .

Dr   Last year?

Mrs A   Well yes . . three times a week . . I broke it off when Dr X went abroad . .

Dr   Did you get on quite well?

Mrs A   Extremely well . .

Dr   Too well for your husband? He didn't like that . .?

A   No, well, it created, I put it very mildly . . great difficulty . . my wife began to withdraw . . I appreciate of course that this sometimes happens . . but it happened more than was reasonable . . and then finally something happened . . I asked to get in touch with this analyst . . at first she said, yes, certainly she would see me, and then she kept me waiting for two days . . and finally she contacted me about five minutes before she departed on holiday . . and then she said she couldn't after all . . I'm afraid I got rather angry at this . . and what struck me most of all was this . . she was disappearing on holiday for two weeks or so . . she left my wife completely in the lurch, this is from my wife's point of view, she made no attempt to contact my wife and tell her 'now don't worry about this . . I'll explain when I come back' . . and I realised . .

Dr   I know you understand quite a bit about these things . . you have insight . . so you must forgive me if I am very frank with you . . we are not here to be complimentary . . I understand from your notes and one can see that you are very morbidly competitive . . aren't you . . and that seems to come out over again . .

A   Yes . . oh yes . .

Dr   Well don't you see this is a transference situation for you too. Don't you think it is just a jealousy . . you can't stand . . you are told the best thing you could do is to keep out . . it is obvious that you couldn't stand that . . not to be mentioned, your son not to be mentioned . . by the way I notice you say 'my' son, not 'our' son . .

A   I understand that . .

Dr   Of course, it was too much for you . . did your wife want to leave you . . .?

Mrs A   Not at all . . as a matter of fact my husband is quite wrong in this. Dr X and I on many occasions discussed this question of my son . . which is extremely important . . I have always had this trouble with my elder son . . not so much the younger one but the older one . .

Dr   Yes . .

Mrs A   Also the question of my husband . .

Dr   This came up? Even if it, so to speak, was not your husband's business . . but of course psychologically it is, you see . .

Mrs A   Yes

Dr   . . . Treatment of either of you brings out the most acute conflict for the other . . . (to Mrs A) . . you talked a lot about him . .

Mrs A   Yes, it always came from me, it never came from . . this is as it should be . . I brought up the subject . . after my husband got better I became extremely depressed for various reasons . . well anxious . .

Dr   Well why? . . You see it looks as when one of you gets better the other gets worse . . . yes . .?

Mrs A   Yes . . well, I'll put it in a nutshell, we may as well be frank about this . . my husband chose . . we made some friends, we met some people we both became friendly with . . very much younger than ourselves, and he became rather attracted to this particular girl . . and from relying on me 100% during his illness he suddenly upped and went and more or less clung to this girl . . and this of course made me more more anxious through this . . and I was in an awful state . .

Dr   Because . . er . . you were jealous?

Mrs A   Jealous yes . .

Dr   Are you fond of your husband? Would you say you are fond of each other?

Mrs A   Certainly . . I always have been . .

Dr   Also now? This is important for possible treatment . . .

Mrs A   I have never entertained a breakup of our marriage . . never . . and my pure intention to go to Dr X has been and always was . . to get myself on a better level of understanding so that I could make something of my marriage, because through this analysis I found out that I was literally or had been using the marriage as a front, not only my marriage but also the children . . to cover up for something . . I haven't yet found out what it is . .

Dr   Yes . .

Mrs A   . . Anyway, right at the very beginning of my treatment with her, I went to her with the idea that I could no longer be civil to my husband . . I was moody, I was depressed . . I was all the things that I hate . . and this was the actual start of the whole thing . .

Dr   Mmm . .

Mrs A   . . But as we found out during the course of this analysis, this trouble didn't arise through marriage . . if marriage had been the answer this trouble would have resolved itself . .

Dr   Yes . .

Mrs A   . . my background is rather an unfortunate one . . my father and mother were divorced when I was 4, I don't remember my father very well . . I met him on one occasion after the divorce . .

Dr   . . Mmm . .

Mrs A   . . consequently I was brought up throughout my life by a succession of women . .

Dr   Yes . .

Mrs A   . . and women have always been a hazard to me . .

Dr   Yes . .

Mrs A   . . now Dr X felt that my problem is without a doubt with women . . and my husband pooh-poohs this idea and says that my trouble isn't with women, it is with men . .

Dr   Probably with both . .

Mrs A   . . Maybe with both . .

Dr   He doesn't want to be left out . . I exaggerate a bit now . .

A   . . . I have no confidence in Dr X at all . .

Dr   How do you justify that in one word, it is really very difficult . .

A   I'm trying to explain why I am so much against her . .

Mrs A   . . My husband has always talked against, and always laughed against, but I know this as a fact . . that with everyone there is a masculine and a feminine side . . and my masculine side is ill . .

Dr   Yes . . that is a Jungian way of putting it . .

Mrs A   Yes . . and I understand to a certain extent what it means . . I am weak, I am not able to make decisions, I am not able to stand by what I say . . in fact always having to be carried along . . I have never been able to stand on my own feet . . my feelings about the children are not natural feelings, but forced feelings . .

Dr   And you are competitive with men?

Mrs A   There is some truth in that, there is a great deal of truth in that . . definitely . . this obviously in some part originates from my father . .

Dr   Yes . .

Mrs A   . . but my husband then claimed that I saw many more problems than were there . . naturally through an analysis one becomes aware of many problems . .

Dr   And how is the situation now . . you have given that up?

Mrs A   I haven't seen Dr X now since before Christmas . .

Dr   You wish to continue this?

Mrs A   Well part of me obviously does, because I have developed a very strong transference with her . .

Dr   Well, would you and could you, could you afford it and so on?

Mrs A   Yes, as a matter of fact we went through this . . my mother is paying for the analysis.

Dr   Mmm . .

Mrs A   And for quite a while now I have felt terribly, terribly guilty about this . .

Dr   Mmm . .

Mrs A   because it is something I really ought to do myself . .

Dr   This would of course make your husband feel his jealousy if you have three times a week a private analysis which he cannot get . .

Mrs A   I'm sorry to interrupt you, but there is this terribly, terribly important thing which has . .

Dr   Yes . .

Mrs A   . . happened before Christmas, which has literally caused all this strain . . that my husband put his foot down literally and said that if I continued with the analysis he would leave . . this is really the crux of the matter . . I stopped it, that is why primarily I stopped going . .

Dr   I understand that . .

Mrs A   . . because I didn't want him to leave . .

A   I do appreciate that, but then you see this strain became quite indescribable . . not only against myself, but also against the elder boy . . who was also under treatment here, although I am glad to say successfully . . I got the impression that my wife began to see more and more problems . .

Dr   (to Mrs A) . . what have you to say to that . .?

Mrs A   Well, the thing that disturbed me . . I came home and we used to discuss what went on . . well this obviously was wrong because I was getting tied up . .

Dr   Mmm . . I said this to a seminar of doctors here that I was strictly against people talking to their spouses and so on . .

Mrs A   Exactly, this is what Dr X suggested some months ago. She said: 'You will have to cut off psychologically from your husband'. So then I was keeping it all inside of myself . . and then of course the problem arose, and this is part of it, I did cut myself off psychologically, and began to feel guilty about it . .

Dr   It is terribly hard for you both, for your husband and also for you to go for months and months without talking about it . . the analyst can say what he likes and you just the opposite . . but what can one do about it? The problem in your case is just so sharp . . .

A   . . . . anybody that was recommended by you I would be perfectly satisfied with . . it is a special problem when we come to that particular lady . .

Mrs A   I originally went to my solicitor who was a very great friend of the family because the situation was getting beyond me . . and he said he would recommend me to somebody . . who in turn recommended me to Dr X . . .

Dr   (to Mr. A) Your wife cannot possibly be objective about this . . even if this lady wasn't the right person . . (to Mrs A) . . you couldn't have your analyst criticised . .

Mrs A   Well, if the criticism was justifiable . .

Dr   Well, if . .

Mrs A   Well, that's another problem I have, I have never been able to come face to face with her and tell her of my doubts and so on . . you see the transference is extremely strong . . also sexually this has come up terribly strongly . . and I feel now between the devil and the deep blue sea . .

Dr   Would it be an idea to separate for a year, and absolutely not see each other . .?

A   If that happened, I don't think we would go together again . . I'm sure of it in fact.

Dr   Would you feel sad?

Mrs A   Well my main objective, my main aim in life is to find myself to such an extent that I can be a good wife to my husband . . I don't want to leave my husband or break up the family . .

A   . . The marriage has never been of the strongest right from its inception . . I think my wife would agree with me . . but we managed to get companionship . . and indeed in many ways considerable fondness . . but through this trouble, since it became acute this strife . . what is it now, four months? . . it has really cut us off . . there is literally a wall between us you see . . and the interesting thing is that since she has not gone to this particular analyst matters have considerably improved, I think she would agree with this . .

Dr   Yes, but obviously not good enough . .

A   Can I just say . . it is not really for me to say, it is for you to say, doctor, . . what my wife might need is something like what I have had, some rather strong psychotherapy . . I don't know whether she is suitable for analysis, I can only judge this by intuition, and I know I am biased . . but this is my honest feeling . . I'm quite sure it would be different if her analyst was somebody I had faith in . .

Dr   I am sure, but *you* don't have to have faith in . .

A   Doctor, there are in fact two people, three people . . my wife gets on very well with my younger son . . my elder son, well, this is the most unfortunate thing . . considerable envy and jealousy between my wife and elder boy . . and he has quite seriously tried to leave home . . this was a gesture I think to me . . because he was saying 'Well, if I can do it, why can't you do it,

Daddy?' . . So there are three people involved . . and the situation has become worse and worse and worse . . . and I can't tolerate this . . I am quite positive that if my wife were treated by psychotherapy . . .

Dr (to Mr A) I don't think you can put your wife under your command, away from this analyst to somebody else . . you can't do that, take her away like a parcel from one analyst to another just because you want it . .

Mrs A . . she actually pushed me to becoming terribly annoyed. She actually said to me on one occasion 'Look, the aggression belongs here — not at home . .'

Dr Yes . .

Mrs A And I couldn't see that . .

Dr You are quite right to interrupt, but I was saying that *he* feels, your husband feels that way . .

Mrs A Yes . . . yes . .

Dr . . that she (the analyst) deliberately pushes your wife against you or away from you . . . . .

(Further conversation . . husband says that if treatment continues with Dr X he will leave his wife . . . .)

This example shows clearly the intimate interrelationship of the disturbance of the whole family and why we do better to look at their plexus as a whole as the primary locus of interacting conflicts. This couple in particular demonstrate amongst other things:

1) how one member's, the husband's, improvement provoked a depression in his wife

2) the resentment and strong reaction on the part of the husband to his wife's changes under her treatment.

3) individual psychotherapy undermined the precarious marital harmony

4) how enormous are the difficulties to treat them now as a couple with any hope of success.

The diagnostic value of this one interview is impressive and typical.

GROUPS OF MARITAL COUPLES

I shall discuss these groups here, although essentially they belong to the groups which are formed for specific purposes of treatment and have no other contact in life which will be illustrated in Section II by the different forms of the group-analytic group. Groups of marital couples really belong to groups formed in view of their common problems. As the common problem concerned here has to do with the family I include them here.

A similar type of group with common problems which I saw years ago in the U.S.A. consisted of parents of schizophrenic children.

These couples came together to discuss the problems as they arose in their common situation and as they were affected by them. The therapist told me that to his astonishment these parents, members of the group, though not treated at all for their own sake had yet lost a good number of their own neurotic symptons. I was less surprised than he was about this result.

Groups of marital couples are life groups in our present sense insofar as each couple live together and share their problems together. On the other hand the different couples are strangers who have no connection in life with each other and who should not form such connections. In that respect they are a hybrid of a group-analytic group and a family group. Such a group is called together by the therapist to the consulting room, they meet regularly for a set time, an hour and a half, and it is in many respects an entire equivalent of the closed group-analytic group. Some special points about them: I think that these couples must be serious in their intention to preserve their marriage, they must – like other groups – exercise discretion, not meeting outside or knowing each other – they are simply married couples, instead of individuals who meet for the purpose of treatment. My own experience in supervising such groups has been quite favourable and I understand they are generally quite helpful. It is possible that groups of marital couples could also usefully be formed if, by contrast to the above, they are considering divorce, or should from all the circumstances at least separate, but apparently cannot come to a decision without psychological help.

SECTION II

THE GROUP-ANALYTIC GROUP

CHAPTER 3

Diagnostics

THE FORMATION OF GROUPS FOR THE SPECIFIC PURPOSE OF TREATMENT

When forming a group specifically for treatment, patients who have no connection in life with each other are called together. Neither should they develop such contacts during treatment, or, for that matter, later. In these groups we are thus operating *outside* the life situation, with people who are strangers and share only the therapeutic situation. As our model we take the group-analytic group in its various forms.

The patient either comes on his own initiative or is referred to us by another doctor, often a psychiatrist. We meet him first either individually or in a group. Presently we shall deal in more detail with both methods of the initial interview.

Preliminary Information

Before we see the patient, we can elucidate a number of facts by questionnaires. This saves time and allows us to concentrate on the most important living features and impressions during the first interview.

Dynamic Use of Tests and Questionnaires

At this stage tests may be given. There are so many tests with which I am not familiar enough to judge them, but I have been favourably impressed with the MMI test. The thematic apperception test is also valuable, especially for comparing results after a period of treatment with the initial ones. I myself have had personal experience with the Rorschach test. I know this is under a cloud from the point of view of the statistically oriented psychologists because of being too

27

unreliable or too much dependent upon the interpreter. Personally I think that this is inevitable. We can never be free from interpretation in the whole field of psychotherapy and psychopathology and to my mind the great merit of the Rorschach test lies in the fact that it is interpretative and yet furnishes some more objective data which form a check on one's interpretation and guide it. The particularly interesting feature of the Rorschach test is that it stresses formal elements: whether the testee is impressed by large or small figures, whether he sees the obvious, whether he is attracted by colour or by movement and so forth. Such formal components are not usually sufficiently observed in the psychotherapeutic situation. Be that as it may, we will not enter further into the method of psychological testing, without in the least denying its potential value.

The questionnaires I have in mind have usually been specifically devised in view of the particular situation. Thus I used a question-naire at Northfield which was specifically attuned to the military situation and the whole atmosphere of that hospital. Such a relatively simple questionnaire fulfils the following points: firstly the prospective patient can furnish all the *objective data* of his life circumstances, of his family, his profession etc. so that we have them complete and need not further question him. The second and main part of such a questionnaire is to get a *preliminary picture of the patient's attitudes,* while it also makes him an *active co-operator* already in this phase. The patient is asked to write in his own way, briefly or in more detail, as he likes, on such points as: What are, *from his point of view,* the reasons for coming to see us? This includes of course questions as to what disturbs him or others; how he feels about all this himself. I then find it useful to ask him to write on *his own ideas* about his condition, *his own theory* as it were of his disturbance, and furthermore *his expectations,* in particular *how does he think these conditions can change* and how is this change to be brought about?

As already indicated, the patient enters in this way into an active discourse and contact with the therapist, and one can get a very good picture of his condition and his attitude. Naturally one will have to concentrate on these same points again when seeing him, but one will find that it is a great help to have studied the preliminary question-naire and the ideas which the patient conveyed here.

Pictorial Profiles: A Tool for selection

At the Out-Patient Psychotherapy Department of the Maudsley

Hospital I used a different approach. The patients had, in a routine way, already been bombarded by various tests according to the different psychiatrists they had originally seen, the standard procedure being the Cornell Index. For this reason I did not add yet another questionnaire but found that I could use the Cornell Index information and translate it as it were into pictorial and more dynamic form. A number of examples will follow by way of illustration. Before seeing the patient, I went through the Cornell Index filled in by him and noted every point without exception in the way illustrated. I drew a little man or a little woman schematically and placed the complaints as expressed by him onto the different organs or regions of the body in a schematic way: I made a rough division, putting the complaints of a purely physical kind all on the right hand side in red, and those which in their very nature were mental or psychological — descriptions or complaints referring to mental functions — on the left side, in black, but have not followed these up systematically. More important are the qualitative characteristics. Complaints are to some extent a result of the questions raised by the Cornell Index Questionnaire, so is the wording of certain complaints, a product of standardised questioning on the mental side. The dynamically oriented psychiatrist, in particular the experienced psychoanalytically trained psychiatrist, will appreciate that in this way one gets a good picture of the type of anxieties, of the characteristic psychopathological constellation (paranoid, depressed etc) or the erotogenic zones which are outstanding, of the typical forms of anxiety and the levels of regression in terms both of id-impulses and ego mechanisms. For the rest, I hope that the illustrations will speak for themselves and I will have only to say little about each.

Figures 1 and 2 are fairly characteristic and represent the most frequent type of picture one gets.

Figure 3 by contrast is striking by the paucity of symptoms recorded.

Figure 4 by contrast to the following two, 5 and 6, shows a predominance of mental complaints and even the physical complaints are likely to be connected with anxieties, for instance, cold sweats, and particular worries, such as underweight.

Figures 5 and 6, on the contrary are heavily weighted on the physical side and seem to confirm that this is not a favourable symptom constellation for psychotherapy. The form of treatment recommended to a patient was not of course based on the questionnaire alone, but on the following interview and clinical judgement (apart from no. 5 who did not turn up for interview.)

Figure 7 in turn abounds in mental manifestations so that a certain detailed psychopathological formulation could tentatively be made, based in part on the interview; it was also noted that the patient showed very rigid character defences.

I thought it was worth publishing this method as it shows that even a static and mechanical questionnaire, (I am sure very complete to the statistician's delight), can be transformed into a graphic and dynamic picture. Furthermore, it might well be that this technique, or a similar one, could be used for more systematic research in the conventional sense of this word.

THE INITIAL INDIVIDUAL INTERVIEW

The initial interview will be greatly helped by the fact that contact has been made in writing and a preliminary picture of the patient been formed. First of all, one need not worry about those of the objective data which one already has; secondly, the enquiry into the patient's attitude and the psycho-dynamic picture is guided as it were, but not prejudiced by what one has already noted. During this interview one can naturally observe the patient's contact, his way of communication and understanding, his motivation — a very important element — his capacity for insight as he has already acquired it, or shows himself capable of acquiring it by the way he looks upon the intercommunication with the therapist as well as upon his defences. Facts will emerge which have to do with his current life situation, his family, his *complexus.* One will also be able to note any special problems which arise. After this, it should be possible to arrive at a preliminary interpretation of the case as follows

1) Personality and psychodiagnostic dynamics
2) Conflicts — predominantly intrapsychic or interpersonal
3) Outlook and basis for resolution of these conflicts
4) Special observations, if any.

This first individual interview can as a rule be confined to one occasion, though it is desirable not to allow any pressure to interfere and not to have a fixed limited time (such as a half hour or an hour) but to let it take the time it takes. It is however, not often necessary

NAME

AGE (young)

SEX (F)

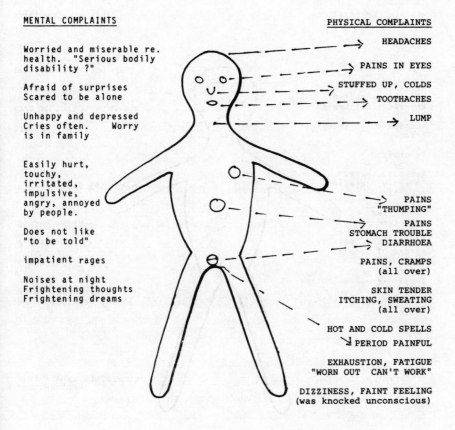

MENTAL COMPLAINTS

PHYSICAL COMPLAINTS

Worried and miserable re.
health. "Serious bodily
disability ?"

Afraid of surprises
Scared to be alone

Unhappy and depressed
Cries often.   Worry
is in family

Easily hurt,
touchy,
irritated,
impulsive,
angry, annoyed
by people.

Does not like
"to be told"

impatient rages

Noises at night
Frightening thoughts
Frightening dreams

HEADACHES

PAINS IN EYES

STUFFED UP, COLDS

TOOTHACHES

LUMP

PAINS
"THUMPING"

PAINS
STOMACH TROUBLE
DIARRHOEA

PAINS, CRAMPS
(all over)

SKIN TENDER
ITCHING, SWEATING
(all over)

HOT AND COLD SPELLS
PERIOD PAINFUL

EXHAUSTION, FATIGUE
"WORN OUT CAN'T WORK"

DIZZINESS, FAINT FEELING
(was knocked unconscious)

Figure 1

N A M E

AGE

SEX   etc.

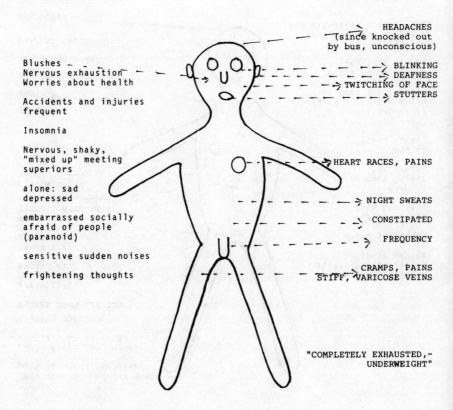

MENTAL COMPLAINTS   PHYSICAL COMPLAINTS

HEADACHES
(since knocked out
by bus, unconscious)

Blushes   BLINKING
Nervous exhaustion   DEAFNESS
Worries about health   TWITCHING OF FACE
                                                        STUTTERS
Accidents and injuries
frequent

Insomnia

Nervous, shaky,
"mixed up" meeting   HEART RACES, PAINS
superiors

alone: sad
depressed   NIGHT SWEATS

embarrassed socially   CONSTIPATED
afraid of people
(paranoid)   FREQUENCY

sensitive sudden noises
                                            CRAMPS, PAINS
frightening thoughts   STIFF, VARICOSE VEINS

                                            "COMPLETELY EXHAUSTED,-
                                               UNDERWEIGHT"

Figure 2

NAME

AGE

SEX etc.

PHYSICAL COMPLAINTS

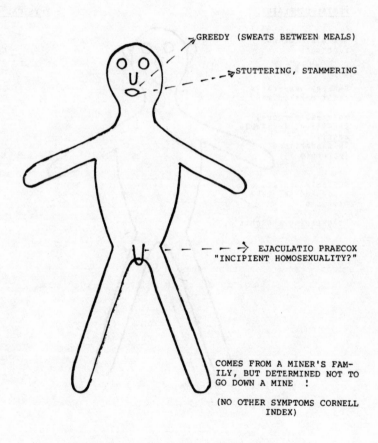

GREEDY (SWEATS BETWEEN MEALS)

STUTTERING, STAMMERING

EJACULATIO PRAECOX
"INCIPIENT HOMOSEXUALITY?"

COMES FROM A MINER'S FAM-
ILY, BUT DETERMINED NOT TO
GO DOWN A MINE !

(NO OTHER SYMPTOMS CORNELL
INDEX)

Figure 3

NAME

AGE

SEX (M)　etc.

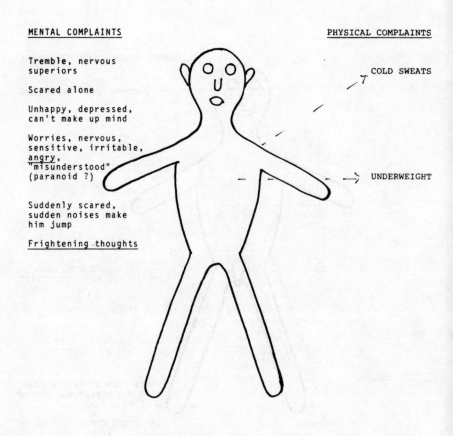

MENTAL COMPLAINTS

Tremble, nervous
superiors

Scared alone

Unhappy, depressed,
can't make up mind

Worries, nervous,
sensitive, irritable,
angry,
"misunderstood"
(paranoid ?)

Suddenly scared,
sudden noises make
him jump

Frightening thoughts

PHYSICAL COMPLAINTS

COLD SWEATS

UNDERWEIGHT

Figure 4

NAME
AGE
SEX

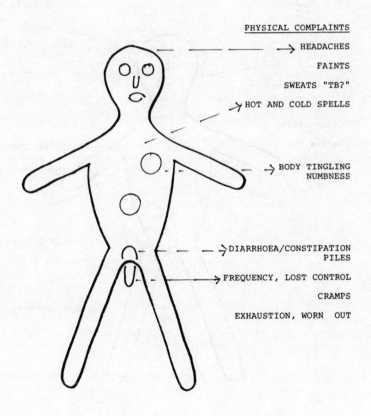

PHYSICAL COMPLAINTS

HEADACHES

FAINTS

SWEATS "TB?"

HOT AND COLD SPELLS

BODY TINGLING
NUMBNESS

DIARRHOEA/CONSTIPATION
PILES

FREQUENCY, LOST CONTROL

CRAMPS

EXHAUSTION, WORN OUT

QUESTIONNAIRE NOT COMPLETED
DID NOT TURN UP - REFERRED BACK

Figure 5

NAME

AGE

SEX etc.

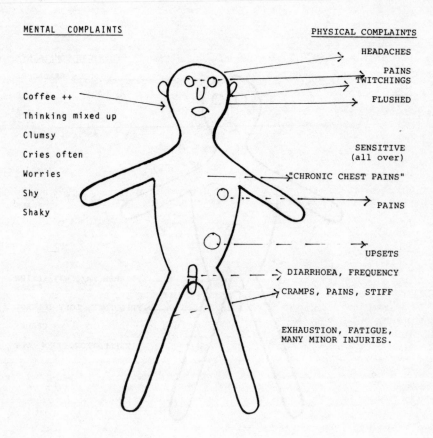

MENTAL COMPLAINTS   PHYSICAL COMPLAINTS

                                      HEADACHES

                                      PAINS
                                      TWITCHINGS

Coffee ++   FLUSHED

Thinking mixed up

Clumsy

Cries often   SENSITIVE
                                     (all over)
Worries
                                     "CHRONIC CHEST PAINS"
Shy
                                      PAINS
Shaky

                                      UPSETS

                           DIARRHOEA, FREQUENCY

                           CRAMPS, PAINS, STIFF

                           EXHAUSTION, FATIGUE,
                           MANY MINOR INJURIES.

SENT BACK
NO WILL TO INSIGHT
PHYSICAL DEFENCE ++

Figure 6

NAME

AGE   (young)

SEX   F

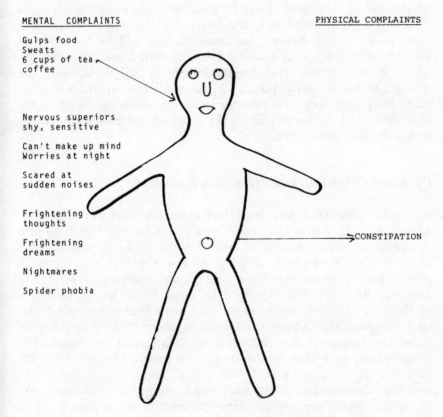

MENTAL   COMPLAINTS

Gulps food
Sweats
6 cups of tea
coffee

Nervous superiors
shy, sensitive

Can't make up mind
Worries at night

Scared at
sudden noises

Frightening
thoughts

Frightening
dreams

Nightmares

Spider phobia

PHYSICAL COMPLAINTS

CONSTIPATION

MONOSYMPTOMATIC BREAKTHROUGH: Spider Phobia
Oedipal. Primal Scene (Parents' Sleeping arrangement)
Only child. Total Sex Repression, Hy. type.
Technical problem: Rigid character-defence.

Figure 7

to extend such an interview beyond an hour or an hour and a half. I have occasionally settled the whole problem satisfactorily in such a 'first' interview, requiring no further therapy, though in these cases there was particularly good mutual contact. It might take two or more hours, but it can be done.

ASSESSMENT AFTER TREATMENT

At the end of treatment it will be possible to have certain statistical data about his attendance, regularity, or the opposite and the duration of the treatment; important factors will be his mode of leaving, his condition as compared to the initial one, the changes, which were observed, the reasons for them, and particularly the changes in his intimate plexus. Again special observations can be made after some time; it is valuable to have a follow-up, based on the observations in the various networks in which the patient moves, as well as his own statements.

INTRODUCTORY INTERVIEW IN A GROUP

We come now to a less usual but exremely interesting method, namely an introductory interview in a group setting. I shall go into this in some detail because of what I think to be its considerable interest. When seeing patients from the start together in a group, the general assumption is that these patients are expected to carry on as a group. By a method described in more detail later, there is a preliminary selection. Experience has shown that one needs about twelve apparently suitable candidates in order to form a group of eight. Let us assume that this selection, this sorting out, has already taken place, and that we start with a group of eight with the intention of carrying on with this group. The question arises as to whether the conductor of this initial group, this introductory, diagnostic group intends to carry on with it, or to pass it on to someone else, say, a registrar. The approach varies accordingly, although the basic elements remain the same. I will go into both possibilities.

Let me first recall my practice during the last year or so at Northfield because it seems relevant. I took, without selection, without preparation and without any prior knowledge about them the next eight patients referred to me and saw them together. I found it hardly ever necessary to change anything, that is to say that I found I could start with any eight patients and continue with them as a group for their total stay in the hospital.

Another similar example took place at the Maudsley Hospital, many years later, under different circumstances. When taking over the outpatient psychotherapy department I found a waiting list of about 25 people who had been waiting for treatment up to two years. I called them all together, and not surprisingly only about half of them turned up, the rest having disappeared. I saw these people together as they came, to give them some treatment and to see how they could be best disposed of. The group attended fairly regularly, the least suitable ones eliminating themselves by reaching some solution in which they could carry on without further treatment. In spite of the very high pressure on new places in the department a few were put onto a more regular form of treatment in groups or individually, but these were very few. The intermediate rest who regularly attended for several months made very good progress and adjustment. A case I remember for example was a woman who had never consummated her marriage in something like fifteen years and now was able to do so and consequently her marital relationship was very much improved. An example of the opposite effect was that of an outright schizophrenic student who left fairly soon, but who, after another year or two, sent me a bill for treatment received in France (a physical sort of treatment which helped him) and insisted that I should pay this.

From this example it would look that under peacetime civilian life conditions one could equally well treat patients as a group together without any particular selection.

Under the National Health Service, at a Teaching Hospital, it is rare, considering a consultant's range of responsibilities, that he himself conducts a group from beginning to end. Far more frequently, what happened was that the registrar who was to take on a group would sit in with me on the first session, and it was made quite clear to the group that he would carry on with them as their doctor. This system worked very well. What the consultant has to have in mind is that the group members do not form too strong a personal attachment to him and he must keep his personality in the background even more than usual.

This applies equally to the preliminary individual interview. This latter I usually conducted alone without the registrar being present. It takes experience, as well as some art to conduct the interview on the right lines between desirable contact, frankness and confidence, yet leaving free the way of germinating transference for the doctor who will take over the group.

Now to the main features of the method I adopted at an initial interview in a group setting. The group were of course strangers to each other, and they were strangers to me. I was a stranger to them. I started, say, with the patient to my left and, one after another round the circle asked them the kind of question which was relevant for all: "What is the matter with you?" "What brings you here?" "What do you feel about it?" and so forth. It is important to create the right atmosphere, to make it understood from the outset that everyone is encouraged to speak, comment and react to what is being said, even out of turn. The group thus comes to life. It is my recollection that this was achieved in every single instance, that not only had I spoken to each one and formed a picture of each, but that some interaction began to take place, often a highly significant one.

It would take too much space to give may examples, but I will at least give some random extracts of one such interview in which some of the episodes which are characteristic for these points are at least sketchily illustrated.

> *A man, whom we will call "M" says:*
> M: I have been a bit depressed lately, and a bit fed up.
> Dr: Yes, you feel fed up.
> M: Yes, I feel I am not going back to my old state, you know, feeling very depressed, but I feel very fed up at this moment.
> Dr: Yes, tell me a bit more about it. Is it to do with your house or what?
> M: Yes, in a way. You know I have explained before that this is a very critical time, and I find that I am not satisfied with things until I think they are really good and very few things I see really are good. Any way this maisonette of mine is having an effect on me and I am extremely irritable with people, usually because they don't seem to come up to my standard, and they don't seem very observant and I find this is very irritating.
> O: What sort of people are doing some work in the maisonette with you?
> M: Oh, it's friends, my mother and father, my fiancée and the fellow next door. I can't explain it really but I feel that no-one is taking the same trouble as I am and I am feeling that I am sort of getting an unfair burden of the worry and concern over it. I am always finding bits and pieces that have been forgotten and no-one seems to notice or bother about it and I seem to resent this.
> Dr: When you felt like this before you weren't under treatment were you? You didn't get a chance to talk about it?
> O: It is not anywhere to the same extent . .
> M: I felt all right before. Quite cheerful and steady, but since I have been doing this decorating I've been getting more and more irritable with people about it, I am disturbed about it and I feel I'm being unfair when I'm unpleasant. I don't really mean to be but I get fed up, I get annoyed, you know, to the extreme.

Dr: Yes that's what I mean — you should now use the opportunity to talk about it so you can get hold of what is depressing you, you see. You see, so far you state only the fact that you get depressed, disturbed, I don't know what about. About what, as far as you know, do you get depressed?

M: I don't know. I think I'm very depressed which caused me to see my doctor. I think that was more or less about worrying whether or not to get engaged. It was a question of I didn't really know whether I wanted to or not, and I wasn't sleeping well as a result. I have often found that I'm thinking very much about something, go to bed and I don't sleep soundly and when I wake up in the morning more or less the first thing that comes to my mind is the problem I was toying with the previous day. It affects my sleep very much.

Dr: Yes, but do you think this has anything to do with your engagement and getting married, wanting to really get married and to have a house?

M: I don't know. I don't somehow think so. No. I just think I worry about myself in many ways. I get disturbed and annoyed, worried because I get irritable with people, and tend to exaggerate things and get irritable and annoyed over small things, and I worry about it because I seem unable at the time to be more calm and collected about it.

F: Plenty of people get het up over small things like that.

M: None of the people that I know seem to have the same interest in what interests me, getting jobs done exactly and well — like I feel I must for some reason. I get a terrific urge to do things perfectly and well. I am not just content with doing things ordinarily like most people would be quite content. It doesn't make me content at all. I had a small discussion the other night in fact. Some wall paper we bought — the chap next door came round to apologise because he wouldn't be able to come round one weekend which was all right, I didn't mind that, and my father and fiancée were round there and he put up a couple of rolls of wall paper and the pattern didn't match very well, and there was some discussion on it. I said I thought it was pretty poor of the manufacturers producing paper like that at 15/- a roll and the pattern didn't match perfectly, and the others seemed to argue with me but I wasn't unduly disturbed by that. I always get the impression that people think me unusual or awkward about things where I feel my opinions are quite reasonable and yet no-one seems to think that. That seems to disturb me a bit as well. I feel that often, you know — when I express an opinion people give me the impression that I've got the wrong idea about things. It doesn't seem to get me anywhere whoever I talk with, — they just think I'm funny, a funny perisher, you know and just don't understand me. It's mainly because I'm so exacting and I expect things just so and they don't understand it . . and just think I'm one of those awkward sort of people, and they let it go at that . . . .

O: Maybe she is quiet because she is worried about you and she senses you are a little bit on edge and she is worried about it.

M: I don't think that is the case, I don't think she is the sort of person who worries about people. I've not known her to be worried about anything except when we first met and then she worried and it was very obvious so I think it would be quite obvious if she were worried about me . . in fact I'm sure she would say something. I get very disappointed myself on these occasions, to think I am so irritable and get so het up over small things and I tend to be unpleasant to people and I think about it afterwards and realise I shouldn't have been like that and then I start to get annoyed with myself for having been awkward and perhaps silly, and this really adds to my annoyance of myself which adds then to the certain amount of annoyance I felt personally towards various people.

G: This is a vicious circle.

Dr: This feeling that you have, is it something to do with wanting everything to be so perfect? The others don't feel it such a lot . .

M: I don't really understand it . . .

This beginning of such a session demonstrates how the conversations get going, the others mix in, how one soon gets a fairly good picture of the persons concerned.

E: I'm sorry I'm late . . I waited 25 minutes for a bus, then two came.

Dr: What happened to you last time? (she had obviously not kept her appointment with me).

E: I had some gastric trouble, indigestion and I felt rather bilious. My husband tried to 'phone you up, he tried to 'phone you up before work, but he couldn't get through.

Dr: Well, it's all right . . I mean I'm glad to see you.

E: No, I must apologise for not letting you know.

Dr: No, it's all right, the only thing is you could — when you get these troubles, gastric troubles or something like this — you could try and come, you see, because, you see . .

E: I felt too sick to come. I couldn't have travelled.

Dr: Well, let's see, we were in the middle of Mr. F. You were about to try something out on us, something to do with standards, I think something . . I think there must be something at the back of it — that's all, that it is something else you know.

F: I sometimes think that the times I'm beginning to feel, you know, that the times I must do everything absolutely right . . I get feelings like that too, really, because I'm often putting absolutely everything into school and there is no other life outside and I feel that if everything else comes into perspective I won't get nearly so worked up about everything else being right, you know . . .

M: I wouldn't say that I'm personally wrapped up in my work or anything else particularly.

F: I know the feeling of wanting everything to be right and getting worked up if you can't sort of do everything you know . . well there is too much work done down there for me to do entirely unaided, although it would probably be best for me to do it myself . . then I wouldn't have any grouses about other people at all etc.

G: Do you think there might be some connection with your parents? Do you think they do the work you really tend to dislike most? I've had a lot of conflicts with my mother — I've never felt that she was, you know, particularly suited to be a housewife or mother for various reasons.

O: Well, you say that other people don't get irritated by the things that you do.

M: Well, I'm sure they don't.

O: Are you sure about this?

M: Yes

O: And you don't think anybody else gets irritated about things like this?

M: Oh yes they get irritated but they forget it inside a few minutes maybe.

F: I don't know, anything besides the wallpaper can you use as examples? . . .

Later on, another patient, X, comes into the conversation . . . .
X: No probably other people who, like you, do a job well feel just as annoyed as you — a couple of years ago my friends had a boat you see . . there were two of them, very keen, and the others were just sort of slap happy. Well, they used to quarrel over it . . a bad friendship . . because two of us sort of split up over that, because between us, two of us didn't care, but me and my friend were sort of perfectionists . .
U: If a job's worth doing, it's worth doing properly . . .
A later piece of conversation:
M: Well, because I think that the attitude of my parents is extremely sort of careless and slapdash and . .
Dr: You mean you want to do better? You suffer from your parents?
M: I don't know what you mean by 'you suffer from them' . .
Dr: Why? You say that the reason you complain about your parents, about your mother in this case, is that she doesn't take enough care and that is the reason why you want to do everything so perfectly.
M: Yes
Dr: How do you mean that?
M: I don't know. I suppose in a way really I feel she is unkind and probably careless — simply because it annoys me if you see what I mean. I get annoyed because I think she is being unkind.
Dr: You get annoyed if she is unkind.
M: Probably yes
Dr: And is that what you feel?
M: On almost every occasion that I get annoyed I feel someone is . . I don't know, I don't think I feel persecuted but . .
Dr: Would it mean then that you don't want to annoy other people?
M: Yes it is probably that . . I like to please people, I like to be kind to people, if I feel I haven't been I get quite disturbed about it.
Dr: But then other people than your mother go on annoying you . .
M: Not to the same extent, no . . .
And so forth.

Somewhat later . . .
E: Oh well I had a stomach ache and diarrhoea and felt dreadfully sick and I was sick earlier in the morning.
Dr: Was it just on that Friday?
E: It was about early Friday morning. There's been a lot of sickness in school. It wasn't because I didn't want to come . . or anything like that.
Dr: Well not so simply. You see we must assume . . we can't allow anything to happen, to be just outside . . either in the body or in the work . . and stop there. Otherwise all the trouble goes out that way . . you see what I mean. I'm not saying that you didn't want to come . . not so simply, but I was saying when you came in that if you can, — even if something is physically wrong with you, or you think it is, if you can come, do come . . even if you think you are too sick and can't . . you see I'm rather impressed . . it is a typical case in question . . you see Miss Y didn't come because she has a cold . . and it would be

very important that she would be here . . wouldn't it? She knows that she can
get a cold when something troubles her . .

E: Did she say that?

Dr: No . . she didn't sit down and say 'I want to get a cold' but she gets
one . .

E: When I was in hospital I heard that theory of doctors several
times . . that you've got a cold because you don't want to go home and visit
your parents and you can develop it into something or other, and I've seen it
develop into a violent case of the 'flu . . where they had to call in an outside
specialist and I'm jolly sure it wasn't caused because this girl wanted to get a
cold and wanted to get the 'flu . . I've seen all sorts of things happening . . I
know illness can be psychosomatic to a certain extent, but I don't think lots are
that are put down to that . . I don't think colds are, I'm sure they are not . .

I hope this extract has given an idea as to how these introductory
groups develop and how, from the start, they are introduced into the
right atmosphere and influenced to look at everything from a
psychological angle, as it affects the whole person. The patient will
also become acquainted with the conditions which he will meet and
has to accept, and with the requirements his participation demands,
if it is to be successful.

It is hoped that this little sketch and excerpts of such an interview
also gives some idea as to *how* these rules and the total culture, the
conditions and requirements, about which we will speak later in
detail, are being introduced. Briefly they are not given as orders,
commands or conditions, but the group is made to understand them
and their significance as the occasion arises.

FROM A PSYCHODIAGNOSTIC EXPERIMENT

Now I will give a short excerpt of a particular experiment which took
place when I was visiting professor at the University of North
Carolina, at Chapel Hill, U.S.A. (1958). The background will be given
as it then was, and I will not transcribe the actual sessions, confined
for experimental reasons to an hour spent with four patients. I hope
that even the samples I can give will show just how much dynamic
information can be obtained in such an initial group session. The
purpose was purely psychodiagnostic and also didactic for the
students who watched the procedure through a one-way screen. Each
week four totally unknown patients were seen together for one hour.
I had no prior information whatever about them. The same patients
were seen by an experienced psychoanalyst and psychiatrist, Dr.
Vernon, individually, each for a quarter of an hour. We kept our
observations apart from each other, and the arrangement was that

the same four patients were first seen in a group and secondly in individual interview during one week, and the other week the other way round. In this way we examined I should say up to 100 patients, and the examples given represent an ordinary cross section.

This is the outline of the original plan:

PROPOSED GROUP DIAGNOSTIC INTERVIEW
During Dr Foulkes' stay in Chapel Hill we are setting up a group diagnostic interview which he will conduct weekly on Wednesday mornings at 10.00 a.m. Rooms 6 and 7 on the ground floor have been booked and a request has been made that a microphone be set up, also tape recorders, so that the proceedings on both sides of the one-way screen can be recorded.

Dr Prange will be in *administrative charge* of this programme as regards selecting or rejecting suggested patients for the group meeting. The intention is that Dr Foulkes will meet with four patients for an interview which will be observed through the one-way screen by third and probably fourth year students, attending men, chief residents and other interested participants. In particular we would want whenever possible to have the residents present who are assigned to the patients being studied in the group.

Patients should be ones who would probably be considered suitable for psychotherapy. They should not show extremes of age and should either all be of the same sex or the group should consist of two of each sex. In general, Dr Foulkes would prefer the presentation of patients who have been fairly thoroughly studied on the in-patient service already although he has no objections to the inclusion of recently admitted patients. If psychological testing has been completed on the patients this is all to the good.

Patients should have the procedure explained to them by the assigned resident along the following lines: "We have a visiting doctor here and we think it would be helpful for you to meet with him. He likes to see several patients at a time. Some of our students may be observing this interview through one-way glass."

Dr Foulkes will conduct the interview for perhaps 45 to 60 minutes at the end of which time patients should be returned to the wards by nurses or students. Dr Foulkes will then move into the observation room and will meet with the group for discussion of what he has observed and what conclusions he would care to make concerning the probable psychodynamics of the individual patients. It is suggested that the remarks made by Dr Foulkes and by any other participants at this time also be recorded on the tape. The intention is to compare the conclusions reached by Dr Foulkes with those already reached by residents and others working directly with the patient in the preceding days or weeks. Residents could contribute their observations on the behaviour of their patients in the group and how it relates to what they already know.

One important aspect of this study obviously is the training implicit in observing Dr Foulkes' work and learning how he makes his conclusions. Another aspect which will be pursued is the research one. Dr Foulkes hopes to compare the group diagnostic conclusions with those reached by the usual method. It should be emphasised, however, that he is more concerned with intrapsychic process and of course with group processes than with diagnostic labels. As part of the research aspect of this programme one or more people will be working with Dr Foulkes in this attempt to compare the conclusions reached. This will probably include follow-up study of patients and each day an attempt will be made to record impressions formed during the morning session.

Important is that a questionnaire to which we both adhered was designed and filled in by us after the group or individual interviews respectively. The experiment was never, to my knowledge, fully carried to a conclusion although it was directed in that respect and partly used, I believe, by the psychologist Dr Hans Strupp and his assistant. Actually I had originally included more subtle questions, but had to leave out a number of them because the psychologists objected to them as not being exactly comparable or measurable.

On the whole there was no doubt about the diagnostic value, nor the didactic value of each such session in anybody's mind. The results, insofar as they were in a sense competitive between the individual and the group method, confirmed what one would expect, — namely, that the group interview was not as reliable in eliciting all or most of the relevant *factual* data of the patient, whereas it was by common consent more productive in *psychodynamic* information which was of importance for selection, prognosis and mode of treatment recommended. Only a small fragment of this material which is in my possession will be used here, mainly in order to demonstrate and illustrate the wealth of information relevant clinically, prognostically and for selection elicited in as short a time as an hour for four patients, or an average of a quarter of an hour for each patient.

In the material selected, please note the particular questionnaire used. The selection contains

1) one example of provisional formulation as given immediately to the students and a short provisional report on each patient which was simpler in form than the later questionnaires.

2) an example of a whole group with one individual questionnaire completed after the group session.

3) four examples, two men and two women, from different groups which show some interesting features. The names are of course fictional and identifiable factual data have been omitted.

PROVISIONAL FORMULATIONS – DIAGNOSTIC GROUP INTERVIEW

Dr Foulkes' remarks to the students who had been watching:

Well, today I must make some general remarks first because they apply to all of the patients and they rather influence the total picture, and limit what one could otherwise expect. I would say that there was a common element in these patients in that they were all women of a more or less conversional hysteric type who in addition are in an on-going treatment situation and transference situation and some seem to me relatively longer treated patients. It is possible to be completely blocked with this type of patient when they are as it were having the upper hand as they all join, although unconsciously, in their resistances. They share this "belle indifference" element of being self contained, and they share the same defensive mechanisms too much, as you could see. Those who have been here last time may notice that by contrast they are very reluctant to interact.† Also they made the worst of the situation in apprehension, at least some of them, which again is infectious. They settled down over this but of course some time elapses before that can happen so they thaw up a bit late. The other element is the advanced, relatively advanced treatment situation which came out quite clearly as an unwillingness really to be involved, not sufficient need to come here and talk and an unwillingness to disclose certain things of which they are clear or think they are clear. I mention this and various other features which make this type of group difficult to become lively. Considering all this they did very well. Now correspondingly I feel at the moment anyhow that what I can hold down and say is not so rich a harvest.

Now I'm not quite sure what the names are, but I think this was Mrs Salter, with the heart, and she came out rather clearly but of course in a limited way. Remember she is on the one hand going into details which are irrelevent from our point of view, how many injections she got and so on, at least in a limited time. On the other hand, as I say, she came out fairly clearly. All of them by the way respond to and are obviously better and helped by treatment; at the same time very much, one feels, settled on a line of rather consolidated resistance and defence and some are quite clear about this, others less so. The wish for reassurance is very strong in all. This patient (Mrs Salter) seems to avoid the real relevance of what she is saying about her life. We couldn't get anything out of her in that respect but instead she focusses on some past situation, one can guess what, but it is characteristic that she neither feels called upon (nor can I feel called upon in any way to encourage her under the circumstances) to tell me more about that so she merely indicates that she has recalled some intimate anxiety producing situation in the past, probably connected with the sexual sphere. This may very well be so and be of quite considerable importance in connection with a certain amount of frigidity and unfulfilled, frustrated excitement. This is more or less guess work from experience. I think she hasn't really changed very much and she is more living on the reassurance that physicians did not find anything than on the positive psychological evidence. She also says that her heart symptoms go on and I think this coincides with her avoiding to link the therapeutic situation up *really* with something which concerns her *person*. I am not at all so sure about the relationship with her husband. The most significant statement she made is that, after all, if it could be cured only by a pill that would be so much better.

---

†This was dramatically expressed by self contained way of their sitting without apparently taking much notice of each other.

Now Mrs Frampton is a different proposition. She is much more involved and much more reacting and should go further; should also qualify for some intensive psychotherapy. Her case came out fairly clearly. She's apprehensive; all of them were. She's better. She seems to have really a good relation to her husband; in her mute way of confirming this she was much more positive that the others with their assurances, but she obviously has caught on to the deeper conflict involved, at least I take it from what she said, that there is more than the stress and strain merely of looking after her mother and so on. There is a conflict around this and fears aroused in relation to both her father and her mother must play a big part. She is obviously in the middle of ways because at the same time she started off by saying it was all this stress and strain, sort of explaining it away. As I see it the resistant attitude is strong and the denial strong and marked in all of them. But I would say she is sort of on the right way to being helped, has obviously been helped already and should if possible go deeper and should be benefiting more and can do with more understanding than she so far has. She is qualified to have more understanding.

Mrs. Waley — well, there's not much problem here. She has anxiety features, hysterical features, is anxious, settles down, probably gave a good show as it were, a good portrait of her general behaviour in social situations, and also in all of her life, I imagine. She is very guarded and possibly something more behind this than I could elicit but it's not very marked, about people, social anxiety as she says. I would say she's quite happily repressing and denying, but she's definitely better and one might leave it with her at that. She's all at peace without too much conflict, wants to go home and she wants to make a better go of things, so that her prognosis superficially speaking is good on an ordinary level. She will be on a deeper level, like the others, quite a difficult proposition.

Mrs Lane — she's of course the most subtle case and the most productive at the moment. At any rate she and Frampton are quite of a different calibre in that way, than the other two. Correspondingly they have also the more open symptoms. She has some anxiety features and certain features of depression, possibly of hypomania as well, but the latter in a very light way, so far as I could make out. Her contact is good, was guarded in her reactions to the others. They all reacted nevertheless, more than one might expect in this situation, from this type. Now, again, she wavered between really realising things and hiding them away by saying 'how sick I am' and so on. There are self-accusing mechanisms in a depressive sense as I said, sometimes she thinks they would be better off without her at home. I think she indicated that she had some marital conflict though she denies it again for obvious reasons. They are all rather guarded of each other. I should think nevertheless her prognosis is definitely good and better still with treatment and as she says she needs treatment. There were two important features I may just mention in connection with her. The one was: she has a great deal of controlled and repressed aggressiveness and hostility which she is not aware of. I indicated it in talking to her. I hope whoever treats her didn't mind that; the other feature was her strange breaking out into this giggle of laughter when asked about her first doctor and her second doctor, so I suspect there is some transference problem going on also, partly responsible why she came into the hospital again.

PROVISIONAL REPORTS AFTER DIAGNOSTIC GROUP

MRS SALTER — DIAGNOSTIC GROUP
Observation Describes her heart attack anticipated by faint a week earlier about a month ago. After medical investigation was sent here. She is concerned in a projective way that the others might be disturbed by listening to her story and correspondingly it turns out later that she herself has some fear of mental contamination. About her general defensiveness see my total comments on this group.
Contact Fair. Towards therapist reluctant. Towards others fair. Later on listens quite attentively.
Inquiry She connects a story of an intimate nature with her attacks which, however, she does not wish to reveal. Her father died of his heart when she was 12. She has still considerable symptoms now.
Psychopathological Some evidence of deeper hypochondriacal apprehension and generally of activity on more regressive levels, particularly oral (Narcissistic and with corresponding readiness to primitive identification). Her insight is only partial. Her feeling somewhat better due to reassurance on the absence of any findings on the part of the physical doctors.
Attitude It is characteristic of her attitude that she would still prefer to be cured by pills.
Diagnosis Conversional hysteria
Prognosis Symptomatic — fair
Psychotherapy Would have to be intensive on analytic lines, preferably individually, but it may be that her attitude and defensiveness are too much in the way.
Comments Uses the transference with her individual doctor as a resistance in this situation.

MRS FRAMPTON — DIAGNOSTIC GROUP
Observation Anxious and apprehensive. She had been afraid of her mind going. She couldn't think or do simple things but she is willing to accept this to be due to stress and emotional strain in connection with a number of illnesses in her near family.
Contact Good towards therapist. Towards others fair.
Inquiry Amongst the various illnesses the most significant seemed to be that of the mother's from cancer of which she ultimately died. She seems to have to some extent acquired some understanding of emotional conflict in relation to her mother's death.
Psychopathological Some hypochondriacal apprehensions as to something being wrong inside her still present. Expressed also doubt and wish for reassurance on the part of her doctor. There is likely a problem of identification with her mother's cancer.
Diagnosis Hysterical state with pronounced anxiety partly of deeper character.
Prognosis Good.
Psychotherapy Should be fairly intensive and prolonged if it is to make a difference to her disturbance at deeper levels. This could be done in an analytic group which might help to approach her strong narcissistic component which at present acts as barrier.

Comments   On transference, etc. see my general comments.
Group Dynamics   She takes in what goes on with the others but seems to be considerably self-absorbed which acts as a barrier to her emotional participation.

MRS WALEY — DIAGNOSTIC GROUP

Observation   Very anxious in the immediate situation. Settles down increasingly with some help. Markedly defensive and reluctant to approach. She tells however that she felt sick since about a year ago but was always easily upset and she had states in which she could not sleep because she had things on her mind which she could not get off.
Contact   Fair. Towards therapist and others guarded.
Inquiry   She seems to indicate that she has chronic apprehension to open up with people which she can overcome only slowly. The doctors helped her a lot by talking to her and she is quite happily repressing now.
Psychopathological   Has always been nervous. Takes after mother. There seemed to be more behind her social anxiety than can be elicited because of her strong tendency towards denial.
Diagnosis   Hysteria
Prognosis   Superficially good. She is better and anxious to join her husband.
Psychotherapy   She offers considerable resistance and is not too well motivated towards an analytic approach.

> *Discussion afterwards disclosed that there had been some psychotic episode but that since she entered the hospital she presented the same picture as above. This had not been elucidated partly for reasons connected with the general setting up of this group (see my general remarks). On the other hand, it is interesting that from the recording a passage emerges which I had not taken in in which she describes how she could not sleep from these compelling thoughts. Had I heard this remark it would have been likely followed up by more probing and might have produced some evidence of the potential deeper disturbance. I had twice remarked 'more behind it' in relation to her social anxiety as well as to her account of her general disturbance, but she did not take this up.*

MRS LANE — DIAGNOSTIC GROUP

Observation   She displays well both her apprehensions in the situation as well as her readiness to be carried away talking. The latter she seems to judge herself as a symptom. She tells a long story of her lack of energy which at one time made her so weak she couldn't even strike a match to smoke which she does a lot and her mother had to feed her and her father and her husband had to turn her in the bed. Psychiatry was wonderful and if she had known three years ago she wouldn't be here now. At the same time, she still later said that she did not realise how sick she was, that she only now knows about her problems and that she has a long way to go. There seems to be a particular feeling shared by the others about having to come here a second time. In this connection when asked about her feelings about her doctors she giggles somewhat out of control but refuses to go into reasons why.

Contact   Good. Towards therapist increasingly positive. Towards others good.
On Inquiry   See remarks above. There are also hints of her taking too many
tranquillisers and she judges herself to be somewhat addicted. Implicitly she
blames her first physician. Depressive features emerge such as increasing apathy,
feeling sometimes that her family would be better off without her (there is some
crying at this point) and there are hints that her coming in coincided with more
depression. She did not talk of drugs in this connection but later discussion with
the doctors discloses that she had in fact taken an overdose of drugs.
Psychopathological   Personality disturbance with depressive features. Early
development connected with mother's alcoholism and also with her relationship
to her mother and father. Denies marital conflict but repeatedly states how
much better doctors understand her than her husband though she thinks that has
now changed. Some tendency towards addiction. Her attitude towards approaching her problems and acquiring insight is good.
Diagnosis   Hysterical personality with depressive features.
Prognosis   Good with psychotherapy.
Psychotherapy   Should be very helpful here on analytic lines either individually
or in group but would likely involve deep analysis of the transference situation.
Comments   Transference seemed here not to have been approached, perhaps
rightly because it would involve considerable working through. The alternative
would seem to be to allow a dependent relationship to persist and use it for
occasional fragmentary help in times of crisis.
Group Dynamics   See my general remarks.

A NOTE ON THE GROUP AS A WHOLE *(one session)*
This group was very interesting in that two slightly hypomanic patients, Miss
Green and Mr Wharton, responded very willingly to talking. This did not impress
Mr Hardern, who is depressed and very retarded, although once or twice he
reacted quite significantly.

However, Mrs James, who is in a totally different state of depersonalisation
and derealisation following a severe traumatic loss, responded after a long
interval and then came in very productively. The group thus became very lively
and rather dramatic, at times almost comical, in the way in particular in which
Mr Wharton echoed all Miss Green said and both of them partly commented on
what Mrs James said.

These three acted at times like a chorus to the very scarce utterances from Mr
Hardern. For instance, when he spoke of having lost his wife they discussed in
between themselves guilt feelings and bad conscience and so on, or when he
mentioned he could not sleep.

An interesting feature was how various communications from one or the other
of these patients provoked responses from the others in quite significant ways
either over facile identification, at other times differentiating them, at other
times bringing forth new material. For instance, from Miss Green that her
condition dated since her father's death, etc.

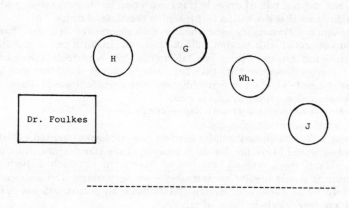

DIAGNOSTIC GROUP INTERVIEW

PATIENTS: Miss Green
            Mr. Wharton
            Mr. Hardern
            Mrs. James

O b s e r v e r s

Clinical (Individual, Group) Observations on which
Statements and Conclusions are Based

QUESTIONNAIRES COMPLETED AFTER DIAGNOSTIC GROUP

Interviewer: Dr Foulkes   *Date:*   *Patient's name:* Mrs J

Manifestations of disturbed behaviour:
a), Overt   This patient was for a long time quiet but she began to talk in
connection with worrying about things which don't happen, she talked readily,
rapidly and incisively. She lost her daughter and the daughter's baby in 19.. in a
car accident. She was never able to get over this, had many bodily complaints,
but the main picture is as follows: her body feels completely changed; at times
she feels quite tall; things are like in a great distance; everything, even colours
and light look different; everything is unreal. She also knows that her mind is
not right.
b) As elucidated   She remembers looking back that she was then normal.
Everything seems far away as if a wall was between her and things. Nothing
seems to make sense. She feels "what are people there for?"' Sometimes she gets
sensations as if people were following her. She hears bells ringing or other noises,
though she realises they cannot be true, as for instance when she heard the baby
cry so vividly that she went into the room to see whether it wasn't there. Before
that time she had many operations, was physically ill, at times could not sleep,
but she still feels now that she was then normal. She now never feels normal at

all. When she first heard of the accident she could not take it in though for a week or so it seemed more real than later. She was more concerned for somebody, to help somebody else. She thinks now she has got all the complexes there are. At times she feels like a couple of people or more. Her dreams have changed to dreams of water, in particular, of things which happened a long time ago and things which have not yet happened. Also of dead people. She sometimes wishes to be dead but realises that suicide is not a solution. In younger years she felt inclined to feel blamed in the family when anything was wrong. She could however get mad at people and used to ao so but now she can't feel that way. She can't have any strong feelings at all.

Developing relationships Good in spite of depersonalisation
Responsiveness strong
Attitude Not without hope of cure
Defensive Mechanisms De-realisation, depersonalisation, denial, dissociation, organic illness
Capacity for insight Good
Estimated intelligence Very good
Verbal facility Very good
Any other features
Comments

Psychodynamic Formulation

Interviewer: Dr Foulkes   *Date:*   *Patient's Name:* Mrs J

Descriptive diagnosis De-realisation, depersonalisation, however within a psycho-neurotic picture not a psychotic picture, reactive to loss of daughter and grandchild which acted as trauma.
Character, personality Now over-shadowed, used to lose temper etc. probably always sensitive, inclined to solve problems with physical illnesses, operations etc. rather than psychological symptoms.
Specific conflict situation Guilt re. daughter and baby in connection with sudden loss. Probably angry reaction underneath that this deprivation has befallen her. Why not for instance the other lady passenger with her baby who escaped unharmed.
Any other comments
Prediction as to course of illness Probably good with treatment

Psychotherapy

Interviewer: Dr Foulkes   *Date:*   *Patient's Name:* Mrs J

1. *Would psychological treatment change the conditions significantly?* YES
2. *What FORM of psychotherapy is recommended ideally?* (e.g. guidance, supportive, manipulative, uncovering (analytic)   ANALYTIC
    Short, intensive, prolonged? Intensive, not necessarily prolonged.
3. *If analytic type recommended, specify:*
    psychoanalytic psychotherapy 2

full psychoanalysis
group-analytic psychotherapy 1
any other
Time (minimal, optimal)
1. 1 year; 2-3 years
2. 3 months; 9 months
Comments on particular features of case concerning, e.g. transference, counter-transference problems, etc.
Contact in connection with her depersonalisation and derealisation experiences is very important. From my experience, group analytic psychotherapy is the method of choice here and such cases have reacted well.
4. *What changes would you expect can optimally be achieved?* Restoration
5. *What factors are anticipated to account for these changes?* Complete process of mourning, accept loss, ventilation, insight into guilt reaction, catharsis.

Clinical (Individual, Group) Observations on which Statements and Conclusions are based

Interviewer: Dr Foulkes   *Date:*   *Patient's Name:* Mrs T

Manifestations of disturbed behaviour:
   a) Overt   Fear of knives. Afraid of panic states which are accompanied by stomach cramps and other physical symptoms. Fear of losing control of impulse to harm people she loves. Started when she was fifteen, twelve years ago, when a girl friend brought an awful looking knife and she had an impulse or thought or idea to stab her mother and now, after repressing this fantasy since then, it has returned in relation to husband and child, since the occurrence of a miscarriage.
   b) As elucidated   She can recognise the physical features from which she occasionally complains as the equivalent of anxiety because that is how she felt in facing exams in former years. She had a happy childhood.
Developing Relationships Fair
Responsiveness Good
Attitude Wishes to understand why she has these harming thoughts about other people. The doctors have said that to find out the reason or cause would help her and she hopes they are right.
Defensive mechanisms Repression, displacement, symbolisation
Capacity for insight Good. Dawning insight that she might have hateful impulses
Estimated intelligence Good
Verbal facility Good
Any other features
Comments

Psychodynamic Formulation

Interviewer: Dr Foulkes   *Date:*   *Patient's Name:* Mrs T

Descriptive Diagnosis Phobia
Character, personality Always liable to anxiety and conversion. Impulsive but

strongly inhibited and repressed, in particular as regards hostile impulses in connection with sex. Strong sex repression.

Specific conflict situation Ambivalence towards loved people clearly connected with sexual symbolisms which is particularly repressed. In oedipal situation likely the father in the centre on a genital level, and on an oral level I would think that the mother, phallic mother, and the castrating mother, the mother who has refused to give her a male cutting organ, is the object of hatred or ambivalence.

Any other comments The particular symbol of the murderous knife expresses her aggressive connotation of sex life in relation to the parental sexual relationship

Prediction as to course of illness Good

Psychotherapy

Interviewer: Dr Foulkes   *Date:*   *Patient's Name:* Mrs T

1. *Would psychological treatment change the conditions significantly?* YES
2. *What form of psychotherapy is recommended ideally?* (e.g. guidance, supportive, manipulative, uncovering (analytic) ANALYTIC
   Short, intensive, prolonged; Intensive, prolonged
3. *If analytic type recommended, specify:*
   psychoanalytic psychotherapy 1
   full psychoanalysis
   group-analytic psychotherapy 2
   any other
   Time (minimal, optimal) (1) and (2) 1½ years minimal — 3 years optimal
   Comments on particular features of case concerning, e.g. transference counter-transference problems, etc.
   No particular features as to transference or countertransference but I would expect the family, particularly the husband, to be strongly involved during treatment.
4. *What changes would you expect can optimally be achieved?* CURE
5. *What factors are anticipated to account for these changes?* Repression lifted, correspondingly insight and working through of conflict situations in transference.

Clinical (Individual, Group) Observations on which Statements and Conclusions are Based

Interviewer: Dr Foulkes   *Date:*   *Patient's Name* Mr B

Manifestations of disturbed behaviour:

   a) Overt Sweats, shows signs of anxiety, restlessness and impulsiveness and even displays his curiosity. He had felt depressed and irritable especially with his family for the last three years. The main complaint is that they don't help.

   b) As elucidated' It took some trouble to get him in here and now he likes to go out soon. He himself was an only child. His parents were critical of him because he did not do well at school and rather scattered his interests and his curiosity. He still tends to do this. He is at times negligent of his affairs as a farmer, hires out business in order to do something else, partly because he could earn more money with this. His disturbance was particularly marked during the last year when he just didn't care. Formerly he used to drink but was able to stop this on doctor's advice.

Developing relationships Good
Responsiveness Good
Attitude Wants to find himself. He wishes to control his behaviour but when emotionally aroused this runs away with him and he admits to some satisfaction in letting go. *Defensive mechanisms* Acting out or rather, living out in life, externalising his conflicts
Capacity for insight Good
Estimated intelligence Good
Verbal facility Good
Any other features His face is striking in being somewhat boyish and immature
Comments

Psychodynamic Formulation

Interviewer: Dr Foulkes   *Date:*   *Patient's Name:* Mr B

Descriptive diagnosis Emotionally unstable immature character
Character, personality Possibly of the passive-aggressive type, is jovial, warm, impulsive and shows very divergent interests. The main emphasis is on his reacting rather from a childish level. His ego in certain respects is weak.
Specific conflict situation Repeats in life, especially in family unresolved childhood conflicts with parents. His internalised ego and superego formation is rather unstable and he still reacts rather childlike in a disturbed situation, created by himself, then that he has internalised his conflict. The obvious specific conflict is the family at present.
Any other comments Made a significant statement as to parents inside him still quarrel. He feels that he takes after both of them and that they quarrel between themselves.
Prediction as to course of illness Not expect deterioration but much better with psychotherapy

Psychotherapy

Interviewer: Dr Foulkes   *Date:*   *Patient's Name:* Mr B

1. *Would psychological treatment change the condition significantly?* Yes
2. *What form of psychotherapy is recommended ideally?* (e.g. guidance, supportive, manipulative, uncovering (analytic) UNCOVERING PLUS CONSTRUCTIVE GUIDANCE AND MANIPULATION.
    Short, intensive, prolonged? Fairly intensive and prolonged.
3. *If analytic type recommended, specify:*
    psychoanalytic psychotherapy 2
    full psychoanalysis

group-analytic psychotherapy 1
any other
Time (minimal, optimal) 1. Min. 9 months; Optimal 3 years, purely group-analytic 2. Min. 9 months; Optimal 2 years, analytic plus constructive manipulative
Comments on particular features of case concerning, e.g. transference countertransference problems etc.
The tendency to act out would tell in the treatment situation, in the transference situation; thus amongst other features would seem to make the group-analytic approach more promising as this tendency would be maintained within the treatment situation and thus would be amenable to analysis.
4. *What changes would you expect can optimally be achieved?* Change of attitude towards himself and family. Solution of his inner inhibitions towards work and fulfilment of his creative capacities. He indicated good capacities with his hands and also considerable interest in writing.
5. *What factors are anticipated to account for these changes?* Correction, in transference, of parental conflict; constructive re work, writing etc. sublimation.

Clinical (Individual, Group) Observations on which Statements and Conclusions are Based

Interviewer: Dr Foulkes   *Date:*   *Patient's Name:* Mrs P

Manifestations of disturbed behaviour:
   a) Overt   Had a cold, looks but turns out not to be schizophrenic. Once cries. Very tense and anxious in session but relaxes later. Laughs once or twice with others in spite of her self-absorption. She looks and feels depressed, increasing feeling of inadequacy and tiredness during last two months but accumulating since a long time.
   b) As elucidated   Considers herself a failure as she can't live up to all her various demands, especially as a mother. There are two people in her, one knows very well what she should do, but one does not feel capable of doing. Much involved in on-going treatment which prevents her from disclosing certain topics. Can speak to doctor but feels more confused at present, in two minds whether doctor is right. Some of the things seem outrageous. Parents were good people but had not much affection. Remembers as child finding other girl's home so wonderful, like a dream. The girl could speak freely about everything with her mother. Always wanted such a home as her ideal aim.
Developing relationships Good
Responsiveness Very good
Attitude Basically positive. Somewhat too self-accusing
Defensive mechanisms Not too strong. Regressive features, splitting
Capacity for insight Very good
Estimated intelligence Good
Verbal facility Good
Any other features
Comments

Psychodynamic Formulation

Interviewer: Dr Foulkes   *Date:*   *Patient's Name:* Mrs P

Descriptive diagnosis Hysterical personality with depressive features
Character, personality Over-conscientious, cannot live up to ego ideal. Destructiveness not too marked.
Specific conflict situation Centred around early mother relationship. Clash between high ideal claims and guilt feelings re opposing tendencies especially in instinctual sphere. Sexual conflict (?)
Any other comments
Prediction as to course of illness Only fair without treatment.

Psychotherapy

Interviewer: Dr Foulkes   *Date:*   *Patient's Name:* Mrs P

1. *Would psychological treatment change the condition significantly?* YES
2. *What FORM of psychotherapy is recommended ideally?* e.g. guidance, supportive, manipulative, uncovering (analytic) ANALYTIC
    Short, intensive, prolonged? Intensive, prolonged
3. *If analytic type recommended, specify:*
    psychoanalytic psychotherapy
    full psychoanalysis — full psychoanalysis or group-analytic psychotherapy
    group-analytic psychotherapy
    any other
    Time (minimal, optimal) Minimum three months, optimal three years
    Comments on particular features of case concerning, e.g. transference countertransference problems, etc.
    Oral regressive dependency and corresponding fluctuations make considerable demands on the stability of therapist. Tendency of flight into organic illness.
4 *What changes would you expect can be optimally achieved?* Solution of conflicts. Free development of personality. Better emotional balance. Better capacity for enjoyment and work. More satisfactory family life.
5. *What factors are anticipated to account for these changes?* Working through in transference. Insight. Growing satisfaction in life.

Clinical (Individual, Group) Observations on which Statements and Conclusions are Based

Interviewer: Dr Foulkes   *Date:*   *Patient's Name:* Mr Y

Manifestations of disturbed behaviour:
    a) Overt No obvious disturbance. 3 years ago well. 2 years ago 'attack' of diarrhoea, chest trouble. Has been for a year in out-patient treatment, last week came here by himself. Something happened to him as if the roof caved in and he appeared to have been in a panic. He later says that he felt like on a precipice and something unknown to him is pushing him down. About two years ago his

brother died of heart attack, the brother with whom he was very intimately connected.

b) As elucidated About two years ago he had an attack which was variously diagnosed but seems to have been due to gall-stones. He thought at first that it was a heart attack. When he was operated he asked the doctors to look around what else they might find. He describes himself as in constant fear of not succeeding and somewhat of a perfectionist. Fear of losing his mind.

Developing relationships Very good, to therapist and others
Responsiveness Very good
Attitude Good witness. Strong evidence of ambivalent doubt and of a physical tangible disease being suspected. Correspondingly some emphasis on what doctors told him and that the ultimate question should be left for the doctors to decide.
Defensive mechanisms Repression, conversion into organic syndrome, partly basis of unconscious identification, ambivalence covered by apparent submission to authority (doctors).
Capacity for insight Very good
Estimated intelligence Very good
Verbal facility Good
Any other features
Comments

Psychodynamic Formulation

Interviewer: Dr Foulkes   *Date:*   *Patient's Name:* Mr Y

Descriptive diagnosis Psychosomatic manifestations, expression of depressive reaction (wish to make clear here a concept of these manifestations taking actual physical form such as gall stones are characteristically equivalent in my terminology of psychotic manifestations or underlying cathexis in the mental sphere, therefore, psychodynamically and topically different from conversional hysteria reactions).
Character, personality Ambitious, perfectionist, must succeed, underneath anxiety and guilt-ridden, somewhat compulsive character
Specific conflict situation Afraid of punishment for success, may be success a refutation of inner accusations, castration guilt seems to have been stimulated, possibly in the form of dying like brother. Brother's death seems to have precipitated this, at least in part the deep seated guilt reactions. Underlying conflict probably with father, reaction formation to passive homosexual submissive tendencies.
Any other comments Deep seated hypochondriacal situation, illness, somatic illness, or other definite evidence of disturbance would be felt as relief from the panic reaction with which he is threatened and which is operating underneath. The basic formula was found by the patient himself who spoke of self-destructive tendencies and of the fear that something will happen which obviously is unspeakably horrid.
Prediction as to course of illness Without treatment, unfavourable, would expect increasing depressive and anxiety equivalents and reactions over the course of time.

Psychotherapy

Interviewer: Dr Foulkes   *Date:*   *Patient's Name:* Mr Y

1. *Would psychological treatment change the condition significantly?* YES
2. *What form of psychotherapy is recommended ideally?* (e.g. guidance, supportive, manipulative, uncovering (analytic) ANALYTIC
    Short, intensive, prolonged? Intensive, prolonged
3. *If analytic type recommended, specify:*
    psychoanalytic psychotherapy
    full psychoanalysis 1
    group-analytic psychotherapy 2
    any other
    Time (minimal, optimal) 1. Min. 1 year, Optimal 3-5 years. 2. Min. 1 year,
Optimal 3 years
    *Comments on particular features of case concerning, e.g. transference,
counter-transference problems, etc.*
    Psychotic episodes, especially depressive ones might occur during the treat-
ment situation and should be considered.
4. *What changes would you expect can be optimally achieved?* Restoration of
confidence and efficiency on less compulsive basis.
5. *What factors are anticipated to account for these changes?* Insight into
self-destructive tendencies. Reduction of deep guilt problems. Working through.

I include by way of a postscript my own answers to a questionnaire which was devised at the time by Dr Barry Gurland who was
then one of my senior registrars at the Maudsley Hospital. The aim of
the questionnaire was 'to find common ground for operative
definition of terms used in diagnostic interviews for psychotherapy'.

The procedure was 'asking experienced psychotherapists for their
definitions of these terms and how they apply them'.

I think the reader of the present volume will find my answers of
interest still.

THERAPEUTIC RELATIONSHIP *"The therapeutic relationship was described
as good in the notes of the diagnostic interview."* Please define: *A good
therapeutic relationship.*

A flexible range of successful intercommunication. Good emotional
contact, rapport, between doctor and patient. They are on the same
wavelength, understand each other. Fair agreement on respective
expectations (rôles, attitudes).

*What would make you conclude at a diagnostic interview that there
was a good therapeutic relationship?*

1) Feelings in yourself:

I can get somewhere with this fellow. He will deal with difficulties and complications arising in the way I prefer and give no undue trouble (e.g. act out violently, become suicidal or paranoid). He likes and respects me, deserves my efforts in treating him. I am pleased, he is good material with which to work.

2) Your observation of the patient:
I can follow him, he seems to take in what I say and mean. He reacts to this and maintains a desirable degree of co-operation in the face of resistances. He is capable of being frank, can see the point of interpreting, switch his mind, shows capacity for insight (see later). He has positive resources and possibilities of development. If a woman in particular, attractiveness helps.

3) Your observation of the interaction between yourself and the patient
During interview moves *towards* therapeutic relationship. A degree of liking and trust develops. Even if things become difficult there is a foundation of good will and mutual respect which will see us through. Important that 'good therapeutic relationship' is *not* simply an expression of "positive transference".

MOTIVATION *"The patient's motivation towards treatment was favourable".*
Please define: Favourable motivation towards treatment
Sufficient scope for change to take place. Independent, genuine desire for change, serious intent for active participation in treatment, ready to face things, signs of perseverance. Positive resources and aims. There is not too great a need for suffering and other signs of unconscious resistances and defences (character defences) not too great.
What would make you conclude at a diagnostic interview that there was favourable motivation towards treatment on the part of the patient?
1) Feelings in yourself:
Assessment of the above partly based on feeling and intuition. If found positive, feeling of satisfaction.
2) Your observation of the patient:
Weighing up the balance between negative impressions and the patient's potential assets to cope with his difficulties. Probing interpretations and observations of his reactions are tests. Especially concerned with *unconscious* motivation.
3) Your observation of the interaction between yourself and the patient.
Necessary to consider both positive **and** negative transference as source of deception either way. Productive response in relation to

interpretation of negative transference and resonances is specially significant.

RESISTIVENESS. *"The patient was resistive to discussion of his real problems".* *Please define: Resistiveness of marked degree.*

Unconscious opposition to personal approach specially strong. Patient evades, denies, opposes links shown between his symptoms, complaints and his problems. Talks incessantly or else withdraws attention, misunderstands or argues. Has firm non-psychological theories in his mind as regards the nature of his complaints, asks for physical examination and treatment etc.

What would make you conclude at a diagnostic interview that there was marked resistiveness on the part of the patient?

1) Feelings in yourself:

Negative as to accepting him for psychotherapy, may be irritated with referring physician. Wish to explode patient's defensiveness — more likely, though, would analyse why he really came to see me.

2) Your observation of the patient

Interested in his defences and how they work. What does he *really* want? Who is *really* sending him and why?

3) Your observation of the interaction between yourself and the patient

Cooler as contact proceeds. See no reason why I should be interested in him as a person, take him more as an object for study. He is likely more tense and hostile as interview proceeds. Warm up if break through occurs, but do not accept pseudo conversion and submission arising as consequence of challenge.

INSIGHT *"The patient seemed capable of gaining good insight".* Please define: *Good capacity for gaining insight.*

The ability to understand and wish to explore his own motivations, not impeded by prejudice, anxiety, shame or guilt. *Not* to be confused with intellectual grasp.

What would make you conclude at a diagnostic interview that the patient's capacity for gaining insight was good?

1) Feelings in yourself:

This capacity will help my working with him and I am looking forward to it. He will also stimulate me and appreciate my contribution and me.

2) Your observation of the patient

Good "psychological intelligence". Prefers truth, is open-minded and curious. Ready to look into himself, rather than external circumstances, blaming others, stick to projections, etc. Some depth of mind, access to phantasy life and symbolic meaning. Can see more than one meaning, can switch, accept interpretations, consider views opposed to his own, make new experiences, etc.

3) *Your observation of the interaction between yourself and the patient.*

Degree of personal understanding and level of talk moves forward during interview. Relaxation of tensions. Feeling of co-operation. Very important again to differentiate transference from good insight and to determine their dynamic relation. Potential good insight can be paralysed by anxiety, etc. and all depends as to whether this or other barriers can be moved.

CHAPTER 4

Therapeutics

INDICATION, COUNTERINDICATION AND SELECTION FOR PARTICULAR GROUPS

Having followed the preparatory steps which the therapist-conductor has to take with prospective patients, we now follow him in the process of the actual selection and formation of a group-analytic group.

In the first place, quite generally speaking, it would be true to say that group psychotherapy is indicated whenever psychotherapy is indicated. Its range is even broader and participation in groups, whether in the form of activity groups or other forms (encounter groups for instance) may be helpful to anyone. However, we should not underrate the danger of exposing people to such encounters when they could be too sick and the experience might cause mental breakdown.

For our purposes, we are concerned only with a very intensive form of group psychotherapy. In this case, of course, we recommend it only to people who are in need of such intensive treatment, which will usually be relatively prolonged.

In talking about the specific indications and counterindications, we do well to look upon two components separately, namely:

1) the practicability of intensive and prolonged psychotherapy within a group

2) the particular indication for an analytical, uncovering approach.

Our patients have to qualify in both these respects. It is important to look on the individual and his disturbances as they have arisen in the context of his intimate plexus, and not as if they had grown merely from his own childhood experiences now internalised altogether. From this view of neurotic disturbances, as multipersonal ones, it follows that the most straightforward approach would be to the plexus or family respectively. Only when for various reasons this is not possible must we treat the individual concerned outside of his plexus, individually, in a new setting. This can be in the conventional, individual situation, in particular that of psychoanalysis, or in a group-analytic group. In both these situations he will be treated as an individual, in his individual capacity, the only difference (a very substantial one though) being that in the group he will join others for the solution and treatment of his problems. Thus he faces his problems with others in a totally new context and in a new situation very different from any that he has so far experienced.

As a consequence of this new approach group-analytic theory can answer the problem of the "choice of neurosis" which psycho-analytical theory cannot. It is not very helpful to speak of individuals in terms of conventional diagnostic labels and to answer the question of indication and counterindication in such terms. Naturally, there are very clear-cut syndromes where the conventional labels are useful, especially in view of counterindications. This applies to pronouncedly paranoid people, to acutely psychotic patients (except under special conditions which we shall mention later), to acutely depressed or suicidal persons and to anti-social psychopathic individuals.

A point in favour of approaching the patient purely individually is the possibility of observing his personal approach to his problems, his response, his capacity for insight, his motivation and the resources of his personality.

It is undesirable for an analytic mode of treatment if the disturbance is too acute, if the problems for which the patient needs help are pressing ones or when it is clear that he is too involved with other persons for them to keep out. Such persons are frequently better served with a form of treatment which helps them to relieve their anxieties or assists them in a limited way over a particular pressing situation and conflict.

Positive indications for an individual psychoanalytical approach rather than a group one are:

a) when the problem is clearly a longstanding one rooted in early childhood, in short a classical transference neurosis;

b) when the disturbance, (as for instance in the case of perversion, or similar intimate ego and character afflictions) is of such a nature that ventilation and analysis in the presence of a number of people would act as an inhibiting factor.

Some people may be too sick to tolerate a group situation. One should however not overrate this factor. With growing confidence in the group this does not often hold good. Our question really is what is the *optimal* treatment, even though both possibilities may be open.

To consider both essential as well as practical points is always a process of weighing up clinically. Occasionally the problem of the differential selection for individual analysis or group analysis arises. On the whole it may be said that there is a considerable overlap and that with more experience it becomes more and more likely that most problems can be solved in intensive group-analytic groups, provided these take place not less than twice weekly. Where necessary they may be followed by a period of individual analysis.

Prior group analysis saves a lot of time and shortens the individual analysis very considerably if it proves at all necessary. I think the contrary procedure, to follow an individual analysis by a group analysis is less useful. It is applicable mainly to trained psycho-analysts who wish to and should have a full group-analytic experience, although I would not deny that there may occasionally be special indications for it.

The fore-going applies more specifically to ambulant out-patients' groups. Under *in-patient* conditions, certain patients selected in accordance with their problems can very well be treated in groups. In this connection I would like to mention, for instance, the group of acutely psychotic, severely disturbed patients on whom Professor L. Miller de Paiva has reported.† He rightly emphasised that such groups should not be undertaken without special precautions, each patient being under the care of another psychiatrist quite outside the group treatment.

On the whole, and as a broad statement, I would say that group analysis is more frequently indicated and more frequently successful than is psychoanalysis and that it has many advantages over the individual method which have to do more particularly with the transference situation and its dissolution. It can be said from both a theoretical and a practical point of view that group analysis is the place in which to study *therapeutic processes* and to practise them, whereas psychoanalysis is the place to study and treat the psycho-genetic circumstances in particular and to study the *causes* or the origins of neurotic behaviour in the chronological sense.

We come now to the question as to what patients we would select to form a group together in order to work optimally. It must be kept in mind that we do not aim at having a "good" group, but from that point of view rely on the process of the analysis itself.

†*Group Analysis: International Panel and Correspondence* (GAIPAC) Vol. IV/3 1971 and Vol. V/1 1972)

FORMS OF THE GROUP-ANALYTIC GROUP

The main forms in actual practice are the *closed,* the *slow-open* and the *combined* group. What we shall have to say about the group-analytic situation is valid for all these. A few specific differences and problems arise from their particular type, which will be briefly discussed.

The fully *closed* group must begin and end together. Patients who might unexpectedly drop out will not be replaced, except in the very early stages, so that the group might be less than the standard number. It should be very carefully selected. It should be time-limited and all the members be prepared, and moreover reliably prepared, to stay the course. This can usually not be under two years and is difficult enough to establish. It is the essence of a fully closed group that the group starts and ends together as a group. There is obviously no objection that one or other member afterwards has further treatment in a different group, where necessary.

What about a combination of individual and group treatment, the *combined* group? (A combined group meets once weekly and its members meet with the therapist in individual session once weekly or at other regular intervals which should be the same for each of the members.) Franz and Annelise Heigl have studied this particular method and investigated the factors which militate for such combination.†

The disadvantage of combined treatment is the special relationship which each patient has, inevitably, with the therapist, however much it may be possible to bring back to the group what goes on between therapist and each patient. When I applied this system myself, exclusively even for the first few years in private practice, I found that the reasons why the patient wanted to see the therapist by himself alone, or what he brought forth with him alone, were not really valid. These were communications on the boundary between the individual and the group situation, and invariably concerned with intimate and very relevant, mostly oedipal problems. I learned to concentrate my individual interview almost entirely on the question: "Why do you want to discuss this with me alone and not with the others?" and regularly found that to bring it back to the group and eventually to leave it completely to the group was the very best

†*Group Analysis: International Panel and Correspondence* (GAIPAC) Vol. III/3, 1970

answer to the whole problem. This also depends on the increasing experience of the therapist. I personally believe that those who like to combine these two methods in one do so, consciously or unconsciously, because they are not sufficiently safe and secure in the group situation. They need the intimate individual transference of the patient as support for their own countertransferential reasons.

I have already said that I much prefer *twice-weekly groups* to combined treatment. It stands to reason that even in these groups under very special and exceptional or emergency circumstances individual interviews may occasionally be necessary and desirable. This, however, is extremely rare and there is no difficulty about making the group feel aware of what is happening and why in this respect.

We are thus left with the *slow-open group* which has established itself as the most usual form. It has, I think, all the advantages of an intensive analytical group treatment and very few disadvantages. The special problems arising are concerned with the introduction of new patients and preparing the group for this event, that is choosing the right patient at the right moment, and also the termination of treatment of the individuals. This is as it should be. Nevertheless, a group which allows for a very slow turn-over is as intensive in character as a closed group. It often has the same composition over a period of a year or two. A very great advantage is that it can do far more justice to the individual's needs and allow the individual to come into and to leave the group as he is thought fit. In this the conductor and the patient himself have the main decision but the group's feelings can be seriously taken into account. Leaving as well as joining needs special consideration both from the individual's and the group's point of view. If well handled the slow-open group is nearer a closed group than is generally realised, and has great advantages over it. After all, it is very much like life, that is to say, people are not together for ever and ever, but they come and go. There is a constant slow move to which to adjust. The character of the group, over the years, changes; the individual joining benefits greatly by the total level of maturity the group has reached. There is also better provision for people who for one reason or another may not be able to stay the course of the group as fully as they had anticipated doing; this can be taken as it were in the group's stride.

The fully *open group* is one with a rapid change of people. It is only practicable in special group therapy centres as a "living waiting list". If people have a longish time to wait it is better for them to have a provisional go at their problems, to get used to group conditions, make some progress, until they can join a more permanent group. There are problems; there is a tendency for such a group to stay together. This would not be the worst, but as selection is important it must be assumed that people taken haphazardly from the waiting list will not be particularly suitable to carry on as a group. Thus in practical experience, the *slow-open* group has emerged as the standard group. I know that some colleagues do not agree, but I think this is not for rational reasons nor based on real experience. Some prefer closed groups, especially certain rather orthodox psychoanalysts, because they can then treat the total group more along the lines and in the rhythms and phases to which they are used with individual patients. There is some truth in this, but it is not a very good reason for concentrating entirely on closed groups.

Having considered these special conditions, we can say that the principles of the group-analytic situation as described in the following chapter, are valid for all forms of group-analytic groups.

We now come to the actual selection of patients who have individually been found suitable to join a group. We will omit special groups or groups under special conditions, or groups chosen for their special problems, in which case they may for instance be all of one sex, etc. We will concentrate on the usual out-patient group, composed of people who will carry on with their lives, professional and personal, in the ordinary way.

The standard group has 8 members of mixed sex, 4 men and 4 women. One of the most important points to take into account is that their general background is compatible, that they are within a certain range of education, of social background, of intelligence, of age. This is far more important than their formal diagnoses which we prefer indeed to be heterogenous. Another principle is that if possible nobody should· be isolated in any particular respect, as for instance the only single person in a group of married people, or the only Roman Catholic amongst Protestants. It is slightly different with Jewish people in that they are in a small minority in their normal situation inside the population. Obviously a group cannot be ideal, it can only fit approximately. One should try to avoid factors which are likely to lead to unnecessary difficulty. It is advisable to have the sexes half and half exactly; suppose we started with a group of five men and three women, it could happen that one of the women dropped out. The relationship of five to two, which would at least temporarily prevail creates special conditions already. When we have four and four, then it is much easier to keep to this proportion.

It is perhaps best to illustrate the principles of this whole

TABLE 1

Proposed group

Date . . . . Dr . . . .

Name	Age	Sex	Mar. State	Occup.	Intell.	Education	Social Background	Special Features	Diagnosis	Main Symptoms or problems	Previous Treatment
A	28	F	M	Housewife	above average	grammar	upper middle		hysteria	Fear of vomiting	2 yrs.
B	31	F	M	Housewife (secretary)	above averag	comprehensive	upper middle		Anxiety State	Loss of identity	No
C	53	M	M	Designer	above average	university	upper middle		Sex Problems	Sado-masoch.	No
D	24	M	M	Clerical	average	grammar	lower middle		Anxiety State	Panics	Drugs only
E	44	M	M	Editor	superior	university	upper middle		Impotence	Marital	1½ yrs. combined group
F	29	F	S	Fashion	above average	grammar	middle		Anxiety State	Severe anxiety bound up with mother	No
G	38	M	M	Accountant	above average	public school	middle		Anxiety and depression	Social anxiety	No
H	42	F	M	Housewife	superior	public school	middle		Frigidity	Marriage never consum.	No
I	32	M	M	Dental Mechanic	average	grammar	lower middle		Impotence	loss of libido	18/12
K	29	F	S	Teacher	above average	compreh. + training coll.	middle		Depression	Sex ident. conflict family	No
L	43	F	M	Housewife	above average	public school	upper middle		Hypochondria	Panics Marital disharmony	2 yrs twice weekly
M	25	M	S	Civil Servant	above average	University	middle		Depression	Homosexual	No

procedure by a grid of the sort I used at the hospital. I will take an ordinary kind of admixture as one would get it at an out-patient department. The reader can then, with me, look at this grid and see in what way, out of, say, 12, a group of 8 can usually emerge. Table 1 is an example of such a selection sheet. Only the most straight-forward factual data are given. (The column "Special Features" is left blank as certain significant details might be too personal for publication.)

We have a list of 12 people, and the first thing which strikes one is that two of the six women are of a different age group than the others who happen to be all just round about 30. So we would tend to omit Mrs H and Mrs L. Now about the men: Mr C is obviously too old for this group and so is Mr E. The marital status with which we are left is equally divided between the women, two married and two single. In the case of the men, Mr M is the only single one. This, however, is not of decisive importance. He is also one of the two youngest ones of the group.

There is nothing special about the occupations which would militate against the group with which we are left, nor about their education which is pretty evenly divided between grammar school, comprehensive school, public school, university. They are all of above average intelligence, with one exception; as these estimates are not very exact we may say that they are all of good and compatible intelligence.

The social background is of course important; there is nothing striking in this respect and any problems arising will in any case have to be brought out into the open and dealt with analytically.

As I have said before, and as will also be evident from this example, the formal diagnosis is not of great importance, neither are the symptoms in the group which is left. Mr M, who apart from depression has some homosexual problems, is in that respect again slightly isolated, but this problem is not very pronounced in his case, and there are others with sex problems amongst the men as well as the women; for example, one problem of impotence. One might consider leaving Mr M out and replacing him by Mr E. He is a little old for this group but he is slightly better adjusted to the group's general physiognomy. On the other hand Mr E has had some previous treatment. This he would share with Mr I. In such a case we can decide between these two possibilities in the light of other factors. It may even be that one more vacancy occurs so that both could be included. A practical decision in such a case would really depend on what alternative is available. Either of these patients, (M and E) might also be considered for individual treatment, so that one might offer one of them an individual vacancy. I see no particular reason to rule out either of them, but for age reasons there is a slight preference to decide for the younger man, with G, at 38, as senior. Thus D and M would be the youngest members, and not be isolated in that respect.

There are of course sometimes more delicate problems, more difficulties to resolve than the ones on this particular list. I mainly wanted to show here how such a selection sheet operates as I think it to be very useful.

THE TOTAL DURATION OF THERAPY

This naturally varies widely: a minimum for any one individual is one year (that is to say 9 months, allowing for holidays), and the maximum in my experience was 8 years. On a rough assessment the optimal time seems to be 3 years or perhaps 2½ years. In my own groups the majority of patients average about two to three years (about 3½ years if one discounts the drop-outs) of regular attendance, with satisfactory results.

The duration of therapy can rarely be determined beforehand, except in a closed group in which case it may have to be limited to one, two or three years. I should like to add a general admonition from life-long experience of results, my own and those of others. That is that we tend to overtreat: we must in case of doubt err at the moment of decision on the side of terminating treatment earlier rather than later. I shall come back to this point when discussing the termination of treatment.

We should have realistic and not over-ambitious aims, based on careful assessment in each case as to what can reasonably be achieved. When the patient comes near to that point and has had sufficient time to work matters out, we should think of terminating and give him and the group plenty of notice to work this through. This working out the reaction to the ending of therapy is very important.

TERMINATION OF TREATMENT

a) Concerning the Whole Group
The termination of the whole group is no problem: in a closed group

the total duration will be pre-determined, and actual ending will be agreed upon a considerable time ahead; in any case a closed group is likely to have a shorter life span. In the usual slow-open group the group is basically continuing. My last two groups of this kind lasted for something like 16 and 10 years respectively (once weekly at first, but twice weekly for the last 5½ and 4 years respectively) and the end came for my own external considerations. Actually one of the groups was taken over by another therapist, who had been for years sitting in with me as co-conductor, Harold Kaye.

From time to time, after a number of years, (say five or six years) with a slow-open group, I terminated a group and started afresh. The reasons for this were partly external, but internally there was a feeling that even the youngest member had reached a stage in which he could terminate, while some of the older members had become somewhat stale and were not providing the best conditions to receive new patients. There was also, so far as I remember, a feeling on my part of being tired with the particular group, getting bored with it, which must also be seen as a part of the spirit which prevailed in these groups. Under such circumstances I gave the whole group notice of termination half a year or a year ahead and stuck to it. On the whole, terminating a group with this technique is no problem.

b) *Concerning the Individual*

We will now say something about the criteria for termination for the individual patient and of the best way to handle this. The first point I wish to make is that our views of the treatment situation and the termination of treatment are conditioned by the total scale in which we operate and in which we think. For instance, at the psychiatric clinic (not to speak of the military situation), the thinking and working was rather in terms of months rather than of years, whereas in the normal group-analytic situation we think, as already indicated, in terms of two or three years. In either case I have developed from my experience a form of *spiral notion*; namely that a point may be reached by which termination seems well possible, or seems indicated when weighing up all sorts of factors which enter into the situation; if we go on beyond this point, either unknowingly or deliberately, it may be quite a while before a similarly good point for termination recurs.

In terms of brief group psychotherapy we may reach such a point after, say, five or six months; but if we extend treatment beyond this point we may not be able to reach a satisfactory point for termination for another year. In intensive group-analytic psycho-therapy, in proportion, a favourable therapeutic result may be within our reach after a year, to be implemented after three or four months' notice, but if we carry on it may well be three years before we again reach such a point. Similarly in long-term individual psychoanalysis: here again one makes the experience that an analysis which might very well be terminated after two years but is continued beyond this time takes at least another year before it reaches, one hopes, at a higher level of the spiral, a good point to terminate. If we then still continue it might be several years before an analysis reaches an equivalent point.

Returning to the group-analytic situation itself with which we are immediately concerned, we think as in psychoanalysis in terms of years rather than months, and similar conditions apply. It is by no means a bad sign if we extend some cases longer than we had originally anticipated. We do so more often because we take a more favourable view of further development rather than a less favourable one. As already mentioned, I would say from my experience as an overall statement that the therapist errs more often on the side of carrying on too long than for too short a time. One makes experiences in which one can see this with hindsight. Sometimes when external factors helped to terminate treatment at a certain point, when perhaps one felt sorry and doubtful and considered this premature, one finds later on that developments show the patient to have done far better than one had thought at the time. Be that as it may, the result of these considerations is that one cannot give the patient a clear answer as to the total duration of treatment, but one should honestly explain this to him and give him an adequate idea of what is reasonable to expect. It is equally risky to give the patient too short as it is to give him too long a view, because whatever view he takes will influence him very much during the whole course of his treatment. It is wise to be extremely cautious in mentioning dates in advance of treatment, and better to avoid this altogether. The problem can be explained very satisfactorily to the prospective patient if one is always frank and sincere and honest about the facts.

The question of leaving the group arises also in a different respect; it is in the nature of things that a patient will not undertake an obligation to stay the course of a treatment for a certain prolonged period. One would not wish to demand this even if it were realistically possible. In other words, the patient must at all times feel free to leave the group when he decides to do so. If the idea comes to a patient at the wrong time and for the wrong reasons, as part of unresolved anxiety, apprehension, from some need to repeat certain situations, self-punishment, opposition to the therapist and so forth, it is clearly important that the question of termination like any other is subject to analysis before it is implemented. When such developments occur within the on-going treatment situation they must be treated entirely on analytical grounds like anything else.

Fortunately there is, as a rule, a fair understanding between therapist and patient when it is time to consider termination and this should be agreed upon well ahead. I would advise to stand firm on one's decision. Even if one should feel that one has made a mistake, it is better not to waver but to let the patient terminate and let him re-start treatment in another group later on. In this connection one has always to reckon with the invariable resistance of the group to losing a member, for a variety of reasons, jealousy amongst others, when the agreed termination of a patient is interpreted as if he had reached a higher degree of perfection than they have, or has been more successful and so forth.

Sometimes a patient wants to leave and is not willing to wait and analyse the situation. These are fortunately rare instances in my own experience, and when they occurred it was fairly early in treatment. These casualties are referred to as "drop-outs". I will have to say something about them presently; the reader will also find their dynamics illustrated in Section III, Chapter 6, when we deal with different examples as they appear on the attendance sheet.

The rarity of drop-outs in my own experience is probably due to careful selection as well as to dealing early enough and adequately with the situation. In those exceptional cases I had mostly been aware of the problem beforehand but had decided to take the risk. Under these circumstances there was nothing for it but to accept the situation, though we were even then usually successful in throwing sufficient light on the situation analytically. Thus at least the group and I could say that we understood what had happened, which is of general importance in all such situations. The least one should try to do is to understand why one occasionally fails as why one occasionally succeeds.

DROP-OUTS

"Drop-outs" are best defined as patients who attend the group for only a few sessions and leave without the agreement of the conductor. In my experience this happens only very early in their treatment, mostly in the first six weeks or soon after. There is another category of early leavers who leave the group by agreement.

In one of my groups with a life-span of some 16½ years — 918 sessions for 57 members — there were only two drop-outs. A further seven members left prematurely for a variety of reasons, but even these, with one exception, left early in the treatment, mostly in the 12th to 15th session. The main reasons for such drop-outs are faulty selection in the first place, unsuitable matching, faulty technique on the part of the conductor, and the group's particular response to a new member at a particular time. This last cause is not necessarily due to faulty matching on the part of the conducting but rather to wrong timing or insufficient preparation of the group for the newcomer.

It should be noted that these figures for drop-outs are extremely low in comparison even to some outstanding group centres and teaching centres where figures of 30% or 50% of drop-outs have been reported. This is another reason why I have devoted considerable space to the theme of selection of patients.

Naturally dropping out is not only a loss for the individual patient concerned but is also a very disturbing factor for the whole group.

ABSENCES AND HOLIDAYS

Patients are expected to give the treatment priority over any other obligation insofar as possible. In particular they are expected to arrange their holidays according to what is agreed upon in the group. If the patient has to be absent unexpectedly he should inform the therapist or his secretary before the group meeting.

The therapist, in turn, will give as long notice as possible of his own vacations and so far as he can will in this respect fall in with the majority situation of the group members.

These provisos are important in approximating the group as nearly as possible to the ideal situation which is that every member is present at every session. These and many other points which are discussed under the headings *Conditions Set* and *Principles of Conduct Required* in Chapter 5 are essential for many reasons. They also serve to give the patient the right image of the importance attached to his treatment and to his own participation in particular. It is my experience that the more seriously these matters are treated by the therapist, the easier they are to keep as they usually support each other. That is to say that laxity in any particular respect produces laxity in others. It should once more be repeated that these conditions are not imposed upon the patients authoritively but are to be learned in the process itself. In my opinion the seriousness of the conductor's own convictions is imparted to the group and helps the treatment in every respect.

FEES

In private practice there is the question of fees. This is not only a practical matter but like everything else has considerable dynamic significance. On the whole I think fees should be equal for all members of any group. As in psychoanalysis, a patient is responsible for his sessions whether he can be present or not, unless in exceptional circumstances there is a special agreement to the contrary.

Occasionally the strict adherence to these principles has caused difficulties when the decision was not clear-cut whether to charge for a particular session or not. This was one of the reasons why I changed the method of payment to one which is now generally practised at the Group-Analytic Practice in London, as follows. The fee is assessed per year and divided into monthly instalments which are to be paid regularly. This scheme works well and has many advantages in relieving the conductor and the patient from unnecessary conflict in these respects.

CHAPTER 5

The Group-Analytic Situation

INTRODUCTORY REMARKS

The group-analytic situation will be discussed under the following three headings:

1) Conditions Set   These are as the patient finds them. He has no influence upon them and is not consulted. He should have been prepared or at least have been informed about them before joining the group.

Meeting with strangers
Particular form of group
Room and seating arrangements
Circle
Position
Numbers of group members
Duration and frequency of sessions

2) Principles of Conduct Required   This refers to the behaviour which is expected of the patient.

Regularity
Punctuality
Discretion
Abstinence
No outside contact
No "life" decisions during treatment.

3) Culture Promoted   This covers the total atmosphere prevailing, the mores and behaviour, as introduced and maintained in operation by the conductor.

Some of these measures, restrictions, limitations, advices, rules and so forth are of importance for any psychotherapeutic group. Others, as for instance abstinence from physical contact and from private relationships are necessary in particular for the purpose of *analysis,* but are partly valid for any intensive psychotherapeutic group. By

79

contrast to "conditions set", which are laid down by the therapist, "principles of conduct required" are based on the understanding of the group members, and are acquired through social learning in the group so that they will be respected and become a tradition of the group. An example of this would be a patient refusing to avoid physical approaches to or outside contacts with other group members or even entering into intimate relationships with them. The conductor would try to convince him of the undesirability of this behaviour and that to abstain is in his own interest.

CONDITIONS SET

Meeting With Strangers

The patients meet, as strangers, with persons with whom they have no prior relationship or acquaintance in life. The consequences of this are profound and important and will be discussed in more detail under "Principles of conduct required" (no outside contact).

Particular Form of Group

The individual patient either joins an on-going group (slow-open group) or he may start in a newly formed group with others which may either be closed or slow-open. In principle the form of group does not influence the handling of the group-analytic situation or change the way the sessions are conducted.

Room and Seating Arrangements

The *room* should be of appropriate size, neither cramped nor too large, and ideally round or square. It is warm, quiet and adequately but not too brightly lit, preferably with light from both sides or from the ceiling (to minimise glare and shadows). If the room is dark, one can observe that people may hide. There should be no more furniture than is necessary, but a barren appearance is to be avoided; discreet pictures and spare chairs are appropriate. The circle of *chairs* is placed around a small round table; this symbolises a kind of centre of the group, and is also a neutral point to look at. A small table is also ornamental and helps to establish a setting more pleasing than the relatively stark and artificial appearance when there is no table. A large table might create the atmosphere of a board or a committee meeting and it also hides people; thus no table is better than a large one. The chairs are uniform, comfortable and simple. They should not be "club" chairs or real armchairs inviting people to lounge. Chairs must not be fixed, and must be light enough to move. The number of chairs in the circle reflects the number expected; when a member is expected to be absent, a chair is removed (− on attendance chart), the circle becoming consequently slightly smaller. When patients are absent unexpectedly the chair remains empty in the circle (O on attendance chart).

The Circle

The setting in a circle (Figure 8) is important though still not generally observed even in some institutions where group psycho-therapy is a principal method. A circle allows every member to see every other member and the therapist. It offers the best face to face situation where everybody *is* equal.

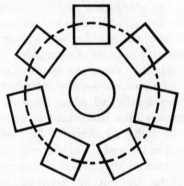

Figure 8

The size of the circle is significant. If the chairs are closer and the number of chairs fewer, patients may feel they are being forced into a more intimate relationship. When a whole group moves their chairs closer together they may be expressing their anxieties.

An example I remember was when one evening it happened that the secretary had put the chairs somewhat closer than usual. When entering the room I had noticed it but did not want to change it. No-one else referred to it except one particular patient who reacted strongly, almost in a paranoid way, as if somebody had secretly done this as an experiment. He said (very significantly), "I am not being forced into closer contact than I wish to be" — and this was after about two years in the group.

Position

Position refers to the particular seats which members occupy in the group session, and any related behaviour. Where people sit and any changes in their choice of seat are meaningful communications. Position is a complex phenomenon, for much depends on the different times of arrival of the different members. Those who come first inevitably determine the position of other members to some extent. (Links are thus established between early and regular time-keeping and seating position.) Changes which may occur at the initiative of one member may nevertheless be significant for the group as a whole. Thus it is clear that position is multidimensional in its determination, containing elements in relation to the conductor, to others and to the total "space" of the group. Moves initiated by certain people, consciously or not, for instance, by coming early, are almost certainly significant in themselves; they may express aspects of the relationship to the conductor and to others, such as opposition or insecurity. One can also disregard the individual to see how much the group as a whole is moving seats, apart from the chain reaction; this usually reflects periods of change.

The conductor by usually taking the same chair sets a feeling of tradition. This makes frequent changes of the patients' positions less likely, as well as more significant when they do occur. The conductor's punctual arrival is also important as regards seating; early patients usually leave his habitual chair for him and if free he sits in it; a patient who arrives early and takes the seat usually occupied by the conductor is thus making a significant communication.

The seat next to the conductor expresses a relationship of particular dependence on him or the need to be protected by him; it may also express a need to be hidden from him. Newcomers frequently tend to choose this position, and with increasing independence move away. Some patients avoid by all means sitting next to the conductor. A patient who habitually sits opposite the conductor may express opposition and a hostile ambivalent relationship. He is also literally more in one's vision and thus receives special attention as well as being more exposed. Proximity or otherwise to the conductor exactly reflects the degree of participation and is related to the strength of the transference.

Sometimes, when there are gaps due to latecomers, the assembling group huddle together, isolating the conductor or putting him in the role of the school master, they demonstrate that they belong together on one side and he belongs opposite. (We and You, Us and Them.) Sitting next to the door may be one way in which a patient expresses his alienation from the group or his desire to leave. Patients with a need to avoid contact may move their chairs out of the circle. Any one group member may express anxiety by shifting his chair, not necessarily away from the group. Very few patients change position during a session, when they do so it is usually in order to express feelings about the group or a particular member of the group, often the person sitting next to them. Sitting on the floor is rarely observed except in psychotic patients − the psychotic patient transgresses conventions that the neurotic can keep. Patients may use seating arrangements to establish sub-groups, either continuing those of a previous session, or those arising out of some informal warm-up activity.

We have given relatively much space to the discussion of the position for a variety of reasons. For one thing, this is a good illustration of the *interdependence* of various arrangements in the group-analytic situation such as regularity, punctuality, the arrangement of the chairs according to the number expected to be present (corresponding to the attendance chart) and the mobility of chairs. The notation registers changes in the group as a whole, expressing for instance unrest by multiple changes in the choice of seats, changes in relation to individuals as well as the conductor in particular. The anxiety or unrest could be quantified for research purposes. The moving of seats can be useful in the interpretation of behaviour. This shows also the reason why chairs should be relatively mobile. For further discussion regarding the dynamic importance of notation, see Chapter 6.

We have shown the dynamic meaning of observable changes in a general way, and now come to illustrate a particular instance, in which changes of the sort mentioned above were analysed. Not only is their dynamic importance brought out clearly but the group's deep knowledge of these happenings is also apparent.

As it happens the excerpt of the session is centred around a dream which is, in itself, of interest. Here are the relevant notations of the changes in seating 'usual':   'changed':

Now the excerpt of the group session insofar as it was relevant to the positional changes in particular. The notes I owe to Harold Kaye who was a co-conductor in this group with myself over a number of years.

G a few minutes late; P 15 minutes late; H came in a moment after most of the others, found her usual chair occupied, hesitated a moment, then went to a chair diametrically opposite. The seating arrangement thus: SHF R S J HK G P H F L, reading from SHF's left. SHF was in his usual position, though the physical arrangement of the chairs was a bit changed as to the original placement and S was sitting in the chair usually occupied by H.

Mrs S started with a dream, which — as the last one — had included the group. In this the identifiable person was R looking very relaxed. Mrs S was dressed in a slip trying to decide which dress to put on. She finally decided on a black one, and just as she put it on, her husband awoke her, so she didn't know what might have happened. She'd being doing a lot of thinking these past few sessions, and had now concluded that she'd killed off her mother and father, symbolically, and taken their places, also symbolically. This was a game she could play with herself: she could have killed one or the other or both, interchangeably and brought them back to life. What she had later evolved was a punishment system, in which she was paying the price of her symbolic murder. On analysis, the black dress, which Miss F (dressed in black) thought of in terms of death appeared to Mrs S to be a formal but not mourning sort of dress. The idea of putting on a dress, but not being sure which one to don, was identified by Miss J as symbolic of Mrs S's search for ego-identity — what sort of person should she be? SHF noted the wish element in the dream — that R who had been anxious in the group was in the dream very relaxed. It was her wish for R, and perhaps also for herself. (Potentially, it's also interpretable having to do with mourning, despite her present denial.) R didn't want to go on until he called attention to H's upset over having her seat taken from her. (Recently she and many in the group have shown a tendency to keep set positions, and this had been discussed in the group.) Oddly enough, she said, she'd been thinking about this whole idea of changing seats, and had concluded this very morning that she might tonight have dared to change position. That Mrs S., toward whom she has a mother transference, occupied "her" seat made it easier to accept a different position. If someone else had been sitting there, she didn't know how she might have felt, but as it was she was very comfortable. (I thought she looked a bit surprised when faced by the fait accompli when she entered.) There was an outburst of talk about seating. Mrs S noted that in her dream there had been a great deal of movement to do with her taking a different position. Miss F had deliberately taken a different chair this evening — one chair closer to SHF than previously. L usually takes a seat two removed from SHF, this time it was on SHF's right. Miss F had been first to arrive, as usual, and deliberately chose a different chair. R took his usual position as to the door (nearest to it) and Mrs S sat next to him. Miss J entering quite early for her sat next to Mrs S. A single seat was thus left for SHF.

Number of Group Members

The ideal number for an intensive group such as the analytical one is 7 members. There are, however, good reasons why we choose the standard number as 8. One of the reasons is that we work with mixed groups and that an equal number of each sex is desirable; furthermore, allowing for people who might drop out or otherwise terminate their treatment and who have to be replaced, and for the fact that, off and on, somebody is inevitably absent, we are in practice often enough left with 7. A group below 5 is too small to work with. It could exceptionally happen that a group is reduced to 5 or even fewer during a particular session, through a coincidence of absences, but this would be an episode with its own dynamic meaning within the total context of the group. In a well-conducted group which is regular it rarely happens that more than one or two persons are absent in any particular one session. The conductor is not included in these figures.

In speculating about numbers one could say the following:

1 person is alone,
2 form a pair,
3 are in a sense the beginning of a group situation.

I have called this the *model of three*. The point is that any one of the three can look not only upon another one but upon the *relationship* between the other two, or between all three of them. With 5, it is for the first time possible for one to be isolated, or in opposition to a compact majority constellation. It is also possible to be in a minority without being isolated, namely in the constellation 3 to 2. Beyond 8, say 9 or 12 or even 15 members, may be a suitable number for task groups, who already have a function to fulfil and are treated as a group in view of their function as a team. Anything much over 15 up to say 70 or 80 is a large group. Anything above that, from 100 onwards to several thousands are thought of as a "mass".

Duration and Frequency of Sessions

The choice of 1½ hours as the standard duration for the group-analytic group was purely empirical but is by common consent widely accepted. I am certain that anything above 1½ hours is too long for the necessary concentration and attention on all sides. Anything less than 1¼ hours is too short to do justice to the members of the group though this depends to some extent on the number of weekly sessions. In groups meeting as often as three or four times a week, I could well imagine that one hour or one and a quarter hours would be quite long enough.

As to the frequency of sessions, once a week is a minimum. They should be quite regular at the same time each week. However I have found twice weekly sessions much more satisfactory. The continuity is much enhanced and only with twice weekly groups have I learned fully to appreciate to what extent the individual sessions hang together. I think the main difference lies in the fact that the interval is only half as long. Obviously the two sessions should be so distributed that they are equidistant from each other. Twice weekly sessions make the whole procedure much more interesting and valuable, but they do not shorten appreciably the duration of the total time taken for treatment. As already stated I much prefer this arrangement to the combined group. I have not myself had the opportunity of conducting groups which meet more often than twice a week. It is possible that holding sessions every other day could have some advantages, though anything more than that would, to my mind, bring the procedure too near to the individual psycho-analytical situation. (This I think, by contrast, should never be less than four and preferably five times a week.) There is no objection to this per se but it changes the character of the group-analytic procedure and induces the conductor to change his expectations and concepts to those he has as a psychoanalyst. I am afraid that this would bring with it some of the potential drawbacks inherent in the strict psychoanalytic situation. The continuation of the transference relationship beyond a certain time and the institutionalisation of the treatment situation is too often out of proportion to its value and purpose. It is a great mistake to think that somebody is the "better analysed" the longer his analysis has lasted. Often the opposite is the case.

However, I have met a number of psychoanalysts, especially in the USA, who prefer to treat their group of patients entirely as if they were one patient in analysis and see them daily. Some confine themselves to group interpretations, others do complete justice to the individual. They are unanimous in stressing the great value or even superiority of this method compared to their own experiences and results of analysis of individuals alone. I have found it a particularly valuable part of group-analytic psychotherapy, that it has such a profound and lasting therapeutic impact in spite of being economical in time and money. The differences between the group method and the individual method are of particular interest also in theoretical aspects.

PRINCIPLES OF CONDUCT REQUIRED

Regularity

The importance of regularity cannot be overemphasised. Not only can the patient not be treated if he is not there, but his absence breaks the inter-communication and continuity of the whole group process. Absences produce gaps in the group's interaction and understanding which are only partly retrievable. Irregularity of attendance means that long periods elapse before the group meets again in the same composition; thus interpretations have a different value because they are not absorbed by the group matrix. Individuals whose attendance is irregular are impeding their progress on their own account too. Fluctuation in numbers is also related to the ability of the conductor to select and to hold patients and above all to the significance he attaches to regularity and to the analysis of the reasons and motivations for absenteeism. Patients are asked to give notice of absence when it is unavoidably anticipated. The conductor should himself be meticulous in his own regularity.

Punctuality

Punctuality is expected as a matter of course. Insofar as the patients should not be late they will inevitably assemble a short time before the beginning of a session. As has been pointed out, this has a bearing on position. It also inevitably leads to conversations, a warming up as it were before the session.

The conductor's punctuality is very important because inevitably the session itself begins with his arrival. The onus of terminating the session is also on the therapist. This should be handled with precision but not with rigidity. A neutral time keeper like an electric wall clock in the room is helpful. As a rule "after sessions" can be avoided apart from natural contact on leaving the premises. Early arrival is rarely habitual and is not generally disturbing. A patient who habitually arrives early may have an obsessional need to be absolutely punctual, never to be late; his relationship to authority figures in this respect will sooner or later be raised in the sessions. Early coming may become a problem if several patients come early, as if by silent agreement. Private "warm up" activity may then occur, either in the group or the waiting room, which will cause sub-grouping with all its dynamic significance. This type of sub-grouping is brought up in the group sessions soon after it occurs.

Latecoming is always very significant; two different types are discernible:

a) sporadic latecoming, or a tendency to arrive late over a relatively short period of time. This is an expression of temporary resistance.

b) chronic latecoming as a character feature. This is a chronic behavioural disturbance, a deep-seated neurotic need which is manifested throughout the patient's life, and whose far-flung ramifications may give rise to widespread symptoms. Classically, in psychoanalytical terms, the patient evinces an anal character and displays strong narcissistic tendencies. The patient rebels against doing something at a specific time when so told. Links are observed between the patient's behavioural pattern and his reactions to basic reality − here to time; he is also likely to have difficulty in completing work on time. Characteristically, the same type of patient finds it very hard to wait for anybody; he would say "I can't tolerate anybody keeping me waiting". In an example we have observed, after a lengthy period during which a patient was consistently late, the group forced the patient's attention to the aggressiveness of his latecoming. Insight into his behaviour was followed by big changes in his personality. As one would expect, besides the benefit to the patient concerned, corresponding effects will be seen on similar tendencies in other members.

"After Sessions" or After-Group Activity

Patients leave the group room at the end of the session, but tend to continue contact with each other down the corridors and into the street. Though meeting outside the group is discouraged, this fleeting kind of contact is inevitable and must be accepted. People travelling together on the same train, or giving a lift to each other in a car, illustrate a degree of contact where acceptability is questionable; it is a borderline degree of contact. A detour to take another group member home, or a drink of coffee together would be significant, not only as behaviour in the group but also as an activity on the boundary of the group and very characteristic of the patient and significant also in other life situations. What is crucial is that boundary activity is brought back to the group; that the patient is not too afraid, too secretive or rebellious to report it and that he has sufficient respect for the analytic agreement. The combination of acting out with withholding information about it from the group is a serious form of resistance, and may become incompatible with continuation of the therapy. I understand that in certain circumstances or in some countries therapists find it difficult or even impossible to stop groups from meeting after the session — for instance to have coffee together. It is reported that quite interesting information can be gained from this and there is no reason to doubt this. According to the principle that any complication should be avoided as far as possible, it still appears to me better to avoid such meetings after the group sessions and I have found no difficulty in England about this, at least in my private groups. As far as the reported observations are concerned, the matters discussed and events occurring at these after sessions were brought back to the group; this is one important point and another is that if such meetings have to be allowed they should concern the whole group. If only part of the group meets, others being excluded, or not participating, I think such licence is definitely undesirable.

The following is an example of a hospital group where the situation apparently allowed the group to meet for a while and to continue their conversation following the termination of the group session, after the conductor had left. It is interesting in various respects and therefore reported here as it was by chance recorded at the time.

(Taken from a recording of the 18th session of Dr G's and Dr P's Group. Dr G is

away on holiday, Dr P in the chair. The following is about five minutes of conversation after the end of the formal session.)

Mary had just been voicing doubts about group treatment being any use, as she was worse rather than better. Dr P ended the session, followed by Clive. The others remained sitting.

Jane *(to Mary)* They're sure to cure you in the end . . they're sure to . . I've known people up in the ward with all sorts of conditions that they've cured.

Cynthia As you said, it strikes me that he's got it all weighed up.

Jane Of course he has — they know just what's the trouble.

Cynthia They get you that much nearer by talking and talking, and they trot out with it.

Jane They're ever so clever — they only come in for the kill at the end, and by golly, do they put you through it.

Mary But I don't feel . .

Jane They're warming up still . .

Robert You don't get that in these groups . .

Jane Well, you do in psychotherapy — they say "We're taking your case history . . ." and you go on and on and on, talking about yourself, and then they start putting you through it, they really wring you out, it's amazing what they do. I don't know how they do it, it's a form of brainwashing. They don't start for a really long time you know, they warm up and warm up until they really turn on the heat. God knows how they do it, I don't.

Cynthia I wonder if they turn on the heat all of a sudden?

Jane Well, I think he's started to put it on Mary somehow, from what I could hear.

Mary I think I won't come next week.

Jane I would if I were you . .

Cynthia Yes, I'm sure they do . .

Robert It must be their policy, not to give you too much information.

Cynthia I think . . isn't there something in the fact that if they say it at the wrong time and too soon, it doesn't properly enter you . . doesn't register.

Jane You've got to be ready for it.

Cynthia You've got to be absolutely ready for it to register . . which apparently a fortnight ago I was!

Jane They lead you on a bit at a time, and they go on saying the same thing until you think you've discovered it yourself. Oh goodness knows how they work, but they've had twelve years of training.

Mary They have to be done first, don't they . . they all have this brain-washing done on themselves.

Cynthia They have to have been psychoanalysed themselves.

Jane Do they?

Cynthia You'd think that they'd discovered that they've got . . . *(Several talking at once, rather indistinct)*

Michael The only fallacy is that the first one had to analyse himself. Freud and Jung analysed themselves, but if they fell down on that self analysis then the whole thing is phoney.

Jane They're not supposed to work on Freud here, it's not a Freudian . .

Cynthia No . . it's Jungian.

Michael Is it a Jungian place?

Mary Isn't Jung . . he's still alive, isn't he?

Jane   No, he died.

Mary   I went to someone just before I came here who'd studied under him at Zurich.

Jane   You've had other treatment before you came here?

Mary   I went to a sort of psych .. oh this lady was to do with the Church .. she was very good really ... (*General laughter*)

Jane   How long did you have?

Mary   I went there for about three months .. then I went to one on the corner of Harley Street .. I always had to pay for these things.

Jane   Gosh, that must have cost you a lot ..

Mary   Oh, it was about, about 11/6d .. a lady psychotherapist .. and I went to this consultant .. he was very nice actually .. he was a Quaker ..

(*Re-enter Clive who had left with the therapist*)

Michael   (*to Clive*): We're having an after-hours session(*General giggle*)

Jane   We do better by ourselves

Mary   Yes, I'm sure if you really want to get better, you can, but I don't think I really want to get better in one respect.

Jane   Oh, I'm sure you do, otherwise you wouldn't come here. I thought at the time I had a subconscious desire not to get better, but that was only a sort of fear.

Mary   Because if I get better, I don't want to lead the same kind of life as I led before ... that's what worries me,.

Jane   But you wouldn't would you?

Mary   I'd feel that I'd have to go to church again if I got better.

Robert   Come to my church with me, we play darts until 10.30.

Michael   If not living at home you wouldn't have to go back to the same place again?

Mary (*doubtfully*)   Not really ..

Michael   You'd only go if you wanted to, surely?

Mary   Yes, but people can recognise certain people that they can work on in the church .. they're really quite ruthless, some of these people, and I'm so weak — I'd be on my guard —.

Jane   That might be a reason for you being like that .. as an excuse for staying away from church.

Mary   I'm sure it is.

Jane   Well, you ought to bring that up next time .... (*Prepares to go*) Was there anyone behind there? (*Points to screen*)

Michael   Expect so.

Mary   Bet there isn't now.

Michael   This is all being recorded — Dr G is going to catch up on this.

Cynthia   Oh, Lord.

Michael   He'll sit down for four days solid, listening to us talking, like Wagner ..

Cynthia   Poor chap ..

Mary   I like Dr P — he's nice isn't he?

Jane and Cynthia   Yes, very nice.

Michael   Comic thing was when I wrote to Dr G and got his name wrong .. I bet they're analysing that .. I used to have a GP in Bristol whose name was Gordon-G, and when I came to write to him I couldn't remember the bloke's name — whether it was Gordon-G or G ..

Mary   How did you spell it?

Michael   I was convinced that this was Gordon-G so I gave him the Gordon-
and then asked him what his name was, and it turned out he's only got the G.
They're probably analysing that one.

Mary   They'll think you've got delusions of grandeur . .

*(Then they all got up and went out slowly, with Michael and Mary talking about
his chance visit to her hospital that afternoon. Some of his voluntary peace
workers were felling trees and demolishing old buildings in the hospital grounds.
Mary said regretfully that she would probably not be there to see him.)*

Discretion

It is naturally assumed that matters discussed in the group remain
confidential within the group and are not talked about to other
people. In practice it is found that the patients do respect each
other's confidences and it is often the therapist who underrates the
trustworthiness of the group.

Within limits it can be anticipated that patients will talk about the
group to a spouse or other person with whom they have a very close
relationship. Patients should understand that on the whole this
should be kept within bounds. The group accepts that this channel of
communication to a near relation is open. It is important that such
communications are brought back to the group. All things considered
this degree of indiscretion is actually helpful. True indiscretion is rare
and is usually the result of faulty selection. One would not offer
analytic group psychotherapy to socially irresponsible or psychopathic patients.

Occasionally, I have, with the knowledge and approval of the
group, seen a spouse together with the patient himself in an extra
session and found this usually very helpful. There were always special
reasons, of suspiciousness or curiosity on the part of the spouse
which could be corrected to the benefit of both and of the group.

The main point in this as in many similar situations is that the
patient concerned is not afraid to let the group know about his talks
and most of the time the group can deal with this very well without
any special interviews.

Abstinence

This concept in psychoanalysis dates back to the time when a
neurosis was thought to be due to sexual malpractice. Before
infantile sexuality was discovered this was thought to be a current
maladjustment, such as coitus interruptus.

It made sense to ask the patient to abstain from such activities during analysis which was then a matter of months rather than years. In this crude sense we do not insist on abstinence today either in psychoanalysis itself nor in group-analytic psychotherapy. What we do insist on is total abstinence regarding intimate sexual relations between fellow patients in the same group.

Abstinence also refers to such tension-relieving devices as smoking, eating or drinking in the course of the session. These we do not allow for good reasons. We ask the patient to abstain from any physical contact, tender or hostile, towards other patients. This has to do with the *suspended action* which is so characteristic for an analytical approach. Here we are in complete contrast with the encounter groups which range from free and frank discussion groups to very intimate group activities. Such socially liberating entertainments may have a considerably loosening effect and even a certain value in the short term by giving a person a push in a desirable direction, but there are also considerable risks attached. These do not occupy us here. The suspended action in an analytic group is also contrary to any emphasis on acting as a means of communication, even literally acting in the sense of psychodrama.

Some otherwise analytically oriented colleagues find psychodrama useful and practise it. I do not doubt that acting or role playing are valuable means of communication; this, however, is very different from an analytical approach. If confined to the session and to the group as a whole, and with the sanction and even on the suggestion of the therapist, it is a different matter. The question is whether it is really necessary. Personally, I find that in the analytic group there is sufficient dramatic action going on between people on deep emotional grounds, and have found "action" unnecessary. During the last war, I experimented with psychodramatic methods and used the material produced for further analysis and consideration.

The deeper issues involved as to whether action as an auxiliary method is (a) necessary, (b) desirable and (c) compatible or not with an analytic approach would lead us deep into theory and should certainly be discussed. I am discussing it here only because it contradicts the discouragement of physical contact during and outside the session.

No Outside Contact

The specific condition for treatment in a group-analytic group is that the patients are strange to each other and have no relationship in life. Members could not feel free to talk to each other in the group if it could lead to consequences in real life. The desirable degree of free communication requires relaxation of the censorship which normally applies in social situations. The group situation must therefore be kept free from social implications, which in addition would stimulate acting out. Only thus is it possible for transference relationships to develop unhampered within the group and for them to be analysed.

We strongly discourage outside contact also because it is liable to lead to intimate relationships with all their neurotic conflicts. The desire for real life relationships among group members is subject to analysis. As absolute compliance cannot be expected it is of importance 'that whatever happens outside is brought back to the group and can thus be analysed.

Here again we know of different attitudes amongst some practitioners; some take a group on prolonged excursions or meet with the group socially outside the session. This is not necessarily incompatible with an analytical approach. The defenders of such a technique would probably say that they can still analyse what happens, that they become aware of many things amongst their patients which they otherwise would not have known. Such a procedure, while it may provide such information and have some therapeutic value, is contraindicated from a strictly analytic point of view. To be at all compatible with an analytic approach it is indispensable that such a social occasion is shared by the *whole* group, including the conductor. Following our principle that it is best to avoid all unnecessary complications, I see no reason why such a procedure should be at all necessary.

No Life Decisions during Treatment

Whilst in treatment it is essential to avoid taking any decisions in life which have serious consequences in reality, quite particularly such as are irreversible, as for instance a change of profession, marriage or divorce. This is a precaution which one cannot overrate. Much psychoanalytical experience has impressed upon us the degree to which motivations and reactions of an infantile, immature character are mobilised during an intensive form of psychotherapy. To act upon them in terms of life decisions is almost without exception disastrous for the patient's own life and future. It is my impression that when this precaution is violated, this is due to the power of self-destructive forces, the unconscious but compulsive need of the patient to suffer and to recreate and reinforce his neurotic misery.

The principles of conduct required which we have here discussed can be at times temporarily as it were "innocently" violated. These transgressions afford the conductor the opportunity to educate the group in these principles and slowly but surely to create their understanding and respect for them. If, however, any one member consciously and consistently refuses to concur with them in any essential part he must be considered as disqualifying himself from this form of treatment.

CULTURE PROMOTED

The features of the situation as we have described it and the way in which they are introduced and handled largely determine the culture of the group. This is not brought about by a particular act on the part of the conductor, although this total atmosphere is the result of his actions and perhaps also to some extent of his personality.

We need hardly do more than enumerate some of the points, such as the cultivation of honesty and mutual respect, tolerance of each other and a certain flexibility and informality. We may say a little more about the kind of verbal communication which is fostered — descriptively I called this early on a *free-floating discussion,* and that is what it really still is. I was then hoping to create the equivalent of free association in the individual psychoanalytic situation and told my first patients that in the group they should associate freely as far as possible, since they were familiar with this from the individual situation. As it is clear that they could not do this, I waited to see what actually happened. There was then, to begin with, no realisation of the degree in which an unforced and in a sense undisciplined discussion amounts to a "free group association", the equivalent in the group to the "free association" of the individual. As usually only one person talks at a time, and the others listen, it takes on, descriptively, more the form of a discussion. The patients soon understand that they need not stick in a logical or systematic way to any particular point as one would do in an ordinary (social) discussion. They should feel free to say at any time what is in their minds, what comes to their minds, what they think and feel.

This is a good occasion to show how important is the form in which one says or conveys anything to a group, especially with the authority of the group analyst or conductor. If one says, for instance: "Say what comes to your mind", it would almost invite patients to talk nonsense. If one says "You can talk about everything you feel fit here, you can talk about everything, however intimate it might be . . ." or some such phrase, it may provoke the idea that the patient is asked particularly to tell secrets or to concentrate almost entirely on communications which would be suppressed socially. It is therefore, as so often, the best thing to say as little as possible and make it understood through the way the communication is treated, so as to be free and spontaneous. What the patients say in fact *becomes* the equivalent of a free association through the way in which it is received and how it is understood. We will have to say more about this when speaking about the conductor's particular contribution to this situation. He acts as a model as well, by the way he himself listens, is tolerant, behaves, and the total tone he sets. He should not become a model in his behaviour as a therapist, which is in certain respects the opposite of what the group member, the patient, is expected to do.

Important too is the fact that the culture, the atmosphere, what is allowed or not, what is expected or not, becomes an established tradition of the group itself. They may still keep away from certain subjects, they will not behave like a "good group", neither should they, indeed, but they should feel free to bring into the open what they really think and feel.

It is one amongst many of the great advantages of the slow-open group that patients benefit from the culture of the total group which is established, so that they often get to the heart of their problems much sooner than they would have done by themselves.

One will find that people develop a certain mutuality, respect and tolerance, and that the group discerns well between what is acceptable indiscretion and what is not. The knowledge that each group member is interdependent with the others sets the group on a very reasonable level of tolerance in these matters. Confidence in the group, mutual respect and confidence in the conductor are naturally of the greatest importance for the whole procedure.

SECTION III

THE CONDUCTOR

CHAPTER 6

The Conductor in Action

PART I

FUNCTIONS AS ADMINISTRATOR

If the conductor is the same person who has taken the preparatory steps we have described then this was of course part of his function. Under other circumstances, the preliminary steps may be the function of a different doctor, perhaps the consultant, and the conductor takes the group over himself only when it first assembles. When the introductory functions are performed by the consultant, it is desirable that the conductor has met the group together with the consultant at the introductory session.

First a few simple but important points which the conductor must observe.

1) Expecting punctuality and regularity, he must himself adhere to these principles very strictly. He should not be early either as inevitably his entrance marks the beginning of the group session. Nor should he prolong the treatment time although he need not be over-rigid in this respect. He can well give himself and the group a minute or so of flexibility at the end of the session.

2) He should himself keep to what he expects from the others, namely to inform the group in good time of any cancellation and to fix his holidays from the beginning so that group members can arrange their own breaks accordingly as they are expected to do.

3) If the conductor has any information himself as to the prospective duration of the group, if it is limited, or as to various questions which concern the patients and might influence their decisions, he should make a point of informing them readily and in good time.

4) The use of drugs should be avoided, except under special conditions, especially in-patient conditions. If drugs are deemed

necessary, they should be administered by a different doctor and not by the psychotherapist himself. These considerations fall under the heading of "dual control". This term is used to describe a situation where a doctor other than the group analyst is involved in the management of the patient. This may be for concomitant physical illness, sometimes for psychosomatic illness or possibly for the same psychiatric syndrome which he is treating in the psychotherapeutic group.

It is important to retain good contact and open-mindedness between the group analyst and the other doctor, in view of transference interactions which can easily arise. There is frequently a different orientation on the part of the physically oriented doctor to that of the psychiatrist. The group analyst should have the ultimate direction in his hands as he is concerned with the whole person. Anything is significant in this respect and the group analyst will be able to look consistently at the psychological side of everything which concerns the patient, be it physical or otherwise. However it is better that the doctors leave each other completely alone rather than collude with the patient's tendency to play one up against the other.

NOTATIONS

Now we come to another aspect of the routine duties of the group analyst which concerns his notations and his notes. It is important that he keeps an accurate record of the group-analytic sessions, a so-called *attendance record*. In the following two charts (1 and 2) examples will be given of the attendance record of two quite different groups, which are very instructive and some observations will be made in relation to them. The forms are on the whole self-explanatory. Basically, it is a list of patients whose presence or absence is noted by the use of symbols. We have also found it important to record latecoming and to differentiate between absences which were expected and agreed and those which were not. It appears to me undesirable to increase the number of symbols used which detracts from rather than adds to the clarity of the record. Extension sheets can be added so that even a group of very long duration can be recorded in its full course. It is clear that such a record is of great importance for any research purposes or statistical investigations. Here we shall concentrate on the more immediate clinical use.

No : **3**

RECORD OF GROUP-ANALYTIC SESSIONS

Place and Time of Meeting :

Private

Type of Group

Mixed Sex. Slow open. All professional people. Psychosomatic ABC but two psychosis, individual treatment, intensive.

Year : **1952**   July – Dec.

Therapist :: S.H.F.
Co: E.J.A.

Session No. 29 1 2 3 4 5 6 7 8 9 30 0 1 2 3 4 5 6 7 8 9 30 0 1 2 23 30 7 14 21 28 4 11 18 25 2 9 16 23 14 15 16 – 17 ....
Day : 1 8 15 22 29 5 12 19 26 2 9 16 5 4 11 18 25 2 9 16 23
Month :: VII   VIII   IX   X   XI   XII

Attendance Quotient :
No. Attended : 6 8 8 8 6 7   5 6 6 7 7 6 7 7 5 8 8 8 8 8 7 8
Total No. : 8 8 8 8 8 8   8 7 7 8 8 8 8 8 8 8 8 8 8 8 8 8

Patients' Names (see back of form for details):

Dr – O
Miss K
Mrs (Dr.) B
Mr. E – N
Mrs H
Mrs N
Mr. S
Mr. L

HOLIDAY

{ HOLIDAY

REMARKS

Symbols :
/ Present.   L Late.
– Absent by agreement.   O Absent unexpectedly.

GAP–H

RECORD OF GROUP-ANALYTIC SESSIONS

No: **III B**

Place and Time of Meeting: Hospital Out-Pat.

Type of Group: Mixed Sex. Slow-open. Average Type: neurotic, middle and lower... No serious treatment of significance.

Year: 1951/52 Oct.–April

Therapist: Dr. W.D. / Dr. C.B.H.

Session No.:	1	2	3	4	5	6	7	8	9	10	11	12	...	13	14	15	16	17	18	19	20	21	22	23	24	25	26	27	REMARKS
Day:	2	9	16	23	30	6	13	20	27	4	11	18		8	15	22	29	5	12	19	26	4	11	13	25	1	8	15	
Month:	October					November						Dec.		January				February				March				April			

Attendance Quotient: No. Attended: 7 6 5 5 6 7 6 7 6 8 6 4 ... 7 6 5 4 5 5 7 3 4 7 6 6 5 5 4

Total No.: 7 7 8 8 8 8 8 8 8 8 8 8 ... 8 8 7 7 7 7 7 7 7 7 7 7 7 7 7

Patients' Names (see back of form for details):

Mr. P.	/	/	/	/	/	/	/	/	/	/	/	/		/	/	/	/	/	/	/	/	/	/	/	/	/	/	/
Mr. N.																												
Mr. St.																												
Mrs. L.																												
Miss E.																												
Mrs. T.																												
Miss I.																												
Mr. B.																												

Symbols: / Present. L Late. – Absent by agreement. O Absent unexpectedly.

Read horizontally, the form records each individual patient's attendance, the character of his participation as it were, in an individual sense, whilst each vertical column gives a lasting picture of the group at any particular session. Looked upon from a holist point of view one gets an excellent bird's eye view of the group. Completed after each session, the record shows who at any stage was a member of the group, who was present at each session and how regular they were, individually and as a group, how the group's composition changed during any particular period of time, what relevant events occurred and so on, a complete historical account of the group. Apart from those who were members from the beginning, newcomers naturally always take the next lower line so that the chart shows at any time how the members stand to each other in terms of seniority in the group. This is particularly relevant in slow-open groups.

I now turn to Charts 1 and 2. Chart 1 is taken from a private group conducted by myself with various co-conductors, and shows the 291st to the 317th session. I want to draw the reader's attention to the regularity of the group, to which I am used. Dr O, the senior member, can be seen to be irregular on his own individual account which corresponded very well to his character and disturbances. He also missed three times without giving notice which in his case corresponded to an attitude: "as I pay for the session, I also have the right to miss a session if I choose." Mrs N finished her treatment after a holiday and was replaced by Mrs C after a convenient, brief interval. Most of the time all those expected were present. Turning now to Chart 2: this was a hospital out-patients' group, of a different social class, not as well selected, and was taken over from one doctor by another, both being beginners in this field. This is not an unusually irregular attendance picture under the circumstances, but the fact is that only very exceptionally are all those present who should be. The number of the group was once down to three out of seven, quite a few times to four out of seven, or to five out of eight. We have two drop-outs, who, characteristically, were both very irregular attenders before they left. After an interval one of them is replaced by a new patient. The fact that there were so many unannounced absences has probably something to do with the class of patient and their habits which is very much in contrast to my group which consisted of highly educated and highly placed professional people.

Even in this relative chaos there was perhaps a hint when absenteeism may have been due to factors concerning the whole group. For instance, in session 20, testing was announced, when seven out of seven were present, and the following week when the testing took place there were only three out of seven present. In session 25 it did at the time appear to us that the irregularity, following on a period of relative regularity, was due to sexual themes having been discussed for the first time in a very personal and intimate way. It must be clear that under the conditions portrayed in Chart 2 the psychodynamics are entirely different from those in a group of more regular attendance. The same people meet each other rarely, if ever; there are continual changes in whom they meet or by whom they may be influenced. This situation arises only too frequently I am afraid under not quite first-rate conducting and care. Even this group to my knowledge was much more regular and had fewer drop-outs than seems to be the case in a number of hospitals, even teaching hospitals, whose percentage of drop-outs appears to be exceedingly high. Such a chart can be looked upon as being the equivalent of a temperature chart in the case of a medical patient. It is particularly important when supervising a number of groups and a number of doctors together.

POSITION CHART

This simply means noting the patients' names as they sit around the table. This record is dynamically significant; it is well worth keeping and especially interesting to those studying the psychodynamics of such a group. The conductor who observes these things and who refers to them at the right moment in the group, when they are relevant, will find how significant they are and will be astonished to find how much the group knows about it. It can be demonstrated that the group have amongst themselves an extraordinary capacity for observing events and interpreting them, although they never come out with these observations unless and until interest is shown in such observations by the conductor. I have myself also operated with a cardboard disc, inspired by a pocket chess board, on which I could retrace the order of arrival which influenced the position in a particular session. For this one needs information from the group concerning early arrivals.

AUXILIARY DEVICES

One-way Screen, Tape- and Video-recording

The one-way screen is a most valuable device for training and research. It has a unique quality as the only method by which observation can take place without changing the observed process. Unfortunately ethical considerations counteract this and it is often felt that the patients should be informed about this installation. Perhaps we ought to be more confident in ourselves that we would not abuse this device, even when the patients are not aware of it. Otherwise this method of observation does change the conditions and thus enters into the transference situation.

Tape-recording is also a valuable teaching and research device but therapy is not furthered by it. It is true that the group "soon forget all about the recording" but this is likely to be due to repression.

I have no personal experience with videotapes for which, however, the same comment might apply.

In the case of either of these methods being operated, use can be made of them by confronting the group on occasion with what was really going on and let them look upon themselves from the outside. I have no doubt that in such a way these methods can at times be valuable. Speaking from a purely clinical point of view one is on the whole better without them. If they are used they must according to group-analytic principles be taken fully into account and must not be glossed over.

CO-CONDUCTORS AND OBSERVERS

A word may be said here about having a co-conductor sitting in. This is of great value for teaching purposes and it has certain advantages. On the whole it is my observation that the group itself is better off with *one* conductor, at any rate *one* should be in charge, and the other be more of an assistant conductor. This second conductor may at times take over and he can make a very valuable contribution and need in no way be given second-rate rank. I prefer a co-conductor to a so-called observer who, if he really confines himself to being merely an observer, is more disturbing and arouses suspicions and certain paranoid apprehensions in the group. It is imperative that the two co-conductors should set aside time to exchange their observations and views. They must strive to overcome personal incompatibilities or acute friction, which are only too liable to be stimulated by the group's influences. Given these precautions, there is a definite value for both in discovering their ways of handling the psychodynamics in the group.

KEEPING NOTES

Let us first say that to make notes during sessions should be out of the question. It is perfectly possible to keep no notes at all without appreciable loss, especially in twice-weekly sessions when the interval is not so great. The continuity or apparent discontinuity of consecutive sessions becomes much more clear in twice- than in once-weekly sessions.

Naturally notes have great value for anyone who wishes to write or otherwise to communicate his experiences. Then it is impossible to do without notes. One loses an enormous amount of detail if one has no notes for lengthy periods. Notes may indeed impede the good memory of the conductor if he relies on them. Notes can represent only a shortened version and a selection, whether conscious or not, of what was going on. It would thus prejudice the conductor if his notes served as his memory. The best time to make notes is as soon as practicable after the group, when his memory is fresh. If he cannot do this until some time has elapsed, he may have more perspective of the session and he can make his selection with greater insight into the processes which have been going on, including his own reactions, so that there is a certain advantage in that.

Another kind of notes are relevant when one is interested at any time in a particular theme or problem or subject, or a particular patient, and deliberately concentrates on this subject. Certainly notes can be useful, but what is quite essential is to give thought after each session and before the next to what was going on. This is not only a very good method of education in this field but it is of current practical importance. It cannot be overrated. The man who really thinks and enquires into what was going on, who examines his own actions and reactions, not only learns much but he is in a totally different position in conducting a group from one who forgets all about it because he was too busy to think about the group, or a patient, between sessions. However, I must add a warning here which may sound a paradox: the thinking-in-the-meantime, with or without accompanying notes, should not under any circumstances prevent the therapist from approaching each group session afresh, each patient individually as well as the group as a whole, as fresh and as unprejudiced as he can. There are exceptions when something has become clear to him which he had not said or not seen before, and he wishes to open up the session with this communication. He may wish to make an announcement, but even then I think he should wait and see and act only in the light of what occurs *now* in this session, and hold his breath about what he has up his sleeve. Yet, again, his memory cannot possibly be too good, insofar as it furnishes him with a living recollection of relevant details which may refer to the last session or two, or even one long past. The resonance in his memory cannot be good enough or spontaneous enough. I hope that what I have said about the apparent paradox concerning the good memory value of notes and on the other hand the need for complete spontaneity will not sound too contradictory. A good and experienced conductor will, without having to think much about it, strike the right note, keep within the right limits as to his participation, communication, as to the boundaries of the group situation and many other things. He has in fact to do much of his thinking implicitly, which is entirely compatible with the highly desirable capacity to be natural and spontaneous.

PART II

THE CONDUCTOR IN ACTION AS A GROUP ANALYST

So far we have dealt with the conductor as an administrator. He has selected the patients, formed the group and created the group-analytical situation as his frame of reference in which he will work. According to our fundamental conviction the situation which is thus dynamically created and maintained, recreated over and over again, this situation determines the whole character and all part-processes of the psychotherapy to take place as it is intended to do. The group-analytic conductor is fully aware of this. He knows that a good number of therapeutic or anti-therapeutic factors depend on the culture he creates and especially on the manner in which he does this. He has made himself into the first servant of the group, into the instrument the group can use, but he has also forged the group, and continues to do so, into the instrument of group-analytic psychotherapy. It is of the greatest importance to realise that in this form of treatment the group itself is the active agency for change. That the conductor forms part of this group situation and is penetrated by it, like any other member, should be clear by now. At the same time there is no mistaking the fact that he is a member with particular functions and of particular significance, in which respects he is in a totally different situation from the rest of the group.

In the following we will consider the conductor as a therapist in the more specific sense. This is a creative activity which needs much intuition. The conductor has to live with the group, expose himself to the currents permeating it and him, try to divine the meaning of what is going on and the relevance of this meaning. Only in the light of such an orientation will he decide on his various interventions, their nature and their timing. His fundamental attitude has been termed *the analytic attitude*. It corresponds to that of the psycho-analyst in the individual situation but with the very great and essential difference that he is aware of operating in a group situation and that his total role is correspondingly different. He has, in my opinion, to think also in different theoretical terms from those of the individual psychoanalytical situation. Of course, the phenomena which we know to exist as psychoanalysts have their counterpart and do occur in the group as well.

On the other hand, certain phenomena are specific to the group situation as I stressed already in my first book in 1948. The range of treatment and the character of therapeutic change to be expected are all transformed in the group. By analytic attitude I mean that the conductor is aware of the psychodynamics as we know them from 50 or 80 years' experience with psychoanalysis; that he is aware of transference, of resistances, of defences, of the structural view point, of the unconscious nature of all these processes, of the importance of symbolic expression. As I have so often said, the conductor ought be an experienced psychoanalyst, though this cannot be reversed; a psychoanalyst experienced in the individual situation would be insufficiently equipped to be a group conductor without special training and experience. Further to the analytic attitude, it is essential to be non-judgemental; above all to be able to listen, and listen again; to cultivate a taste for truth, for inner honesty in the face of confrontation with conflicts. The basic convictions which we hold of neurosis and its roots, of health and the way to it belong to our theory, in particular to a theory of therapy which will not be treated here in further detail.

AIM OF OUR PSYCHOTHERAPY

At this point it will be sufficient to ask ourselves: what do we mean by therapy? In the first place, it seems to me that we wish to enable the patient to change. It is clear that the patient himself must wish to change or, to put it more carefully, he must have sufficient conflict and suffering so that he is in a good disposition for change, that things *have* to change if he wants to be reasonably happy or efficient or freed from the torture of symptoms or from self-destruction, as the case may be. The assessment of this is part of the selective process and has to do with the important element of *sufficient motivation for change* in order to make therapy possible. From the whole group-analytic orientation, as presented in this book, it should be clear that we think that this change involves other people, in particular the inner plexus or complexus of people of which the patient is a part. Therefore in assessing the possibility of change and its degree we have to consider the total constellation within this intimate network, and not only the disposition in the individual patient himself.

We do not wish to change a patient according to our own image, not even to the image of so-called normality or ideally desirable way of functioning within his culture. We do wish to free the patient from those forces which hamper him in the development of his own personality and his own resources. Naturally this must be ultimately compatible with the circumstances in which he finds himself and with the culture of which he is a part. The aim of our psychotherapy is therefore a liberation in the patient's inner psychic life from that which prevents him to change, from his inner blocs, a process of *unlearning* in a sense. Our concern is therefore in the first place the analysis of unconscious inhibitions, restrictions, which are part of the patient's unconscious ego and superego. These processes are of an inner psychological nature, yet I talk of them as permeating the whole group. This is no contradiction when we accept the view that the group-analytic process is in itself based on a shared psychic life. It rests on an intimate network of communication which gradually grows into an organ-like *matrix* inside which all processes take place. The processes are all shareable and increasingly so, and they are all ultimately of an intimate psychological nature. I have therefore spoken of *transpersonal processes* which are located in the total psychological network of the group. The nature of a desirable change in the individual patient tells in his becoming more ready to learn. He continues to learn, to feel, to think, to perceive, in his own person freely — to become himself.

The increase of self-knowledge goes together with understanding others better; the widening of horizons is altogether profound. The basic axis of all these processes consists in *improved communication* and in the increase of range of communication and therefore of understanding and also of information. The group is and remains the active agent and the decisive context whilst the conductor is the guide, – not the leader because he is not going ahead leading the group or the patients in a particular way or in a particular direction but indeed follows the group's own tendencies.

He must be very careful in his inverventions, in what he is, does and represents, because he is likely to be taken as a model, and it is difficult but important to free the members of the group from using this model function of the therapist as a guide for their own development. The tendency, more or less strong in individuals, to behave like him in the ongoing process is a definite resistance and has to be continuously analysed.

As the conductor's interventions are mostly verbal, it is usual to think of them entirely in terms of interpretations. This is not the way in which we shall here consider the situation. Interpretations are important and we shall have to speak about them, but they are only one kind of intervention which fall to the lot of the conductor. He may sometimes have to select the topic of discussion, to draw attention to what the group is trying to gloss over, he may have to confront people, he may have to explain links which are not recognised or the significance of behaviour. He may address individuals or the group. He may ask questions, ask for information and so forth; a great number of interventions which should not all be subjected to the same term interpretation, which has a more specific meaning. When to be silent and when to speak, what to take up, how, when, – to whom remarks may be addressed, all this depends on the conductor's landmarks for orientation, on his perception, conscious or unconscious, of the context.

On the whole we can say that the conductor proceeds from what is manifest to what is latent, what is the underlying meaning. This refers not only to what is said, but also to how it is said, to what happens and why. As to the manifest events it must not be mistakenly assumed that they are understood, or even observed. There must first be a clear awareness of the "what", only then can we come to the questions of "how", "in what manner?", "what implications were operating?" Much interpretation will be necessary to make everyone in the group see and agree to the answers to these questions.

The question *why* does not only mean why ultimately, but also why just now, why just in this manner, why just through him or her, and so forth. On the whole we may say that we proceed *from the symptom* in the widest sense of term *to the underlying conflict* or problem. This process, proceeding from the one to the other, contains many steps all of which together constitute an analysis. Interpretation is only one of the means in the service of this analysis, though an important one.

Analysis is work done in the service of making unconscious meaning or expression conscious. There is a double process going on from below upwards, as it were, and from the surface downwards. We will come back to this when we talk about interpretation more particularly.

All these processes can be looked upon together as if they were translations from one type of expression, from one language to another, from symptomatic and symbolic meaning to a clear understanding of what is at stake. In referring to the total processes we sometimes speak of "translation".

The conductor must avoid becoming too important and must keep in the background. The conductor's built-in importance needs no emphasis. The tendency is not merely to make him into a Transference figure in the true sense of the term, a figure of the past coming alive in the present, but he is also a bearer of very strong emotions arising from his role and special position in the present situation. If he manages to minimise rather than support his significance he will achieve two important purposes. Firstly, it will be easier for him to analyse these projections and delusionary interpretations of his actions and of his person; equally important, perhaps, he will make the group into a more confident and active agent. The group will learn to rely more on itself and be correspondingly more convinced of the truth of its findings. It will be a safeguard against any interpretative prejudgement by anyone including the conductor arising from personal inclinations, school and similar factors. The changes taking place as a result of the interactive processes in the group itself are of a lasting and solid nature.

This keeping in the background must not be confused with principal activity or passivity. I would rather say that the conductor is receptive, he may be very active in his own mind, listening, devoted to what the group is saying or trying to say, very much engaged in his own mind as to his own interventions. He may at times have to be very active indeed. It is a misconception of the principle of keeping in the background when a therapist, often but not always a beginner, literally leans over backwards to be as little actively involved as possible. At the beginning of each session, especially in the early stages, his active help is necessary and indicated. Indeed, the better he fulfils this function the more likely will he be rewarded by the group becoming a more powerful and efficient instrument of therapy.

The conductor should never have to do the group's work unless and until his help is needed. He is much needed in other ways throughout the process, including the use he makes of himself in the group which changes with the situation and in different phases of the ongoing therapeutic process. In minimising his importance as an authoritative parental figure, in infantile and irrational terms as a power ranging from god to the devil himself, he makes a valuable contribution *per se,* reducing the irrational tyranny of the super-ego which is internalised.

What has just been indicated could be understood as a kind of *transference analysis in action,* in contrast to the transference analysis by other means of intervention, in particular interpretation. This expression corresponds to the idea of an analysis of the ego in action meaning by that the psychodynamic action of the ego. The ego processes, like any other, are in my view shared by the total group. They are analysable in the context of the total group interaction by the group themselves as well as by the conductor. Equally, when speaking of translation as making conscious the unconscious, this is meant in a total sense. It does not mean merely the verbal translation of unconscious content into conscious content. It does mean that the total intra-psychic interaction between the different structures of the mind, in particular the *ego, super-ego* and *id* are made visible, are brought to explicit expression in the group, so that the group members themselves can become aware of this on-going dynamic struggle in any one of them, by similarity and contrast. In this way, through the group-analytic process itself, through the work which is necessary to bring all this to manifest or potential expression, they all participate in a therapeutic movement.

INTERPRETATION

I hope it has already become clear that interpretations occur all the time, whether in words or actions, in omission or commission, consciously or unconsciously, and that in this way all members of the group participate in interpretation. They may even try consciously to interpret, similarly to what they see the conductor doing, or they think he ought to be doing. Occasionally, such interpretations can be valuable. On the whole, they are more likely to be suspect for a tendency either to imitate the conductor, taking him as model, or as it were to correct him, to be rivals with him, be co-conductors and so forth.

Here we shall be concerned with interpretations as a practical tool applied consciously by the conductor. The conductor, I repeat, makes many interventions which are sometimes called interpretations, but which should be kept apart from interpretation in the proper sense of the word. Interpretation is a verbal communication by the conductor to the group, or to members of the group, in order to draw their attention to a certain meaning of which he thinks they are unaware but may become aware through this verbal help. He must judge, too, that his interpretation is given at the right moment. The ideal psychological moment is when all or some of the members of the group, or one particular member, seem very near to understanding something, but seem not quite sure. A correct interpretation produces a kind of "Aha! Erlebnis" (experience): that is to say something really "clicks", falls into place and the hitherto concealed meaning becomes obvious.

The conductor should only give an interpretation when he has patiently but in vain waited for this insight to come from the group itself. Even then he may do better to analyse the unconscious defences and resistances which prevent the patients from finding out for themselves. This analysis of resistances and defences implies the unconscious ego's attitudes and the unconscious influence of the super-ego.

Another type of interpretation is the transference interpretation. Insofar as it concerns the conductor himself this should be given mainly by him, and he may well have to be somewhat forthcoming and active in this respect as the group tends to be unaware of the transference process and rather to act it out, to show it by their reactions. The first step is to make the group aware of what they are doing, what they are saying, how they are behaving and only when this is understood *why* they are doing this and that it may have to do with him.

As I see it, any interpretation is in the service of analysis and is dependent on the total insight, on the total interpretation if you like, the conductor himself forms of what is going on in the group at that particular time. We touch here on the problem of countertransference which needs special consideration. Obviously the conductor must first become aware of his countertransference whether in the session, or as it frequently happens, in between sessions, in order to modify not only himself but also his behaviour in the group correspondingly. It is at times indicated for the conductor to analyse his countertransference openly within the group process. This can be extremely important and useful, but must not be made a routine. On the whole, the conductor should be economic with this type of communication. The best hint one can give him as to when such an interpretation on his part may be useful or even necessary is when he becomes aware that some resistance against communication is located in himself, is involving him if not caused by him. Furthermore that he follows the overall rule to interpret only in order to improve and also deepen communication.

Before going into some examples to illustrate some useful or not useful kinds of interpretation, here are some more general remarks: There seems first a difficulty in that the German word "Deutung" which corresponds to "interpretation" was introduced in this context by Freud.† Now *Deutung* has an underlying meaning of a quite specially creative act on the part of the "Deuter" (interpreter), based on specific knowledge on his part, almost of a supernatural kind, by no means open to everyone, but only to the select few who have been initiated on the strength of a quite peculiar ability. In that sense one may talk of a "Traumdeuter" (interpreter of dreams), "Schrift-deuter" (graphologist) or "Sterndeuter" (astrologist). The word "interpretation" as far as I can see has a more rational meaning, thus where one would still say "to interpret" in English, one would never say "deuten" in German, but for instance to show, to point out, to make clear. "Deutung" has a more restricted field but goes deeper, whereas interpretation has a wider field of application but remains more on the surface. It may be worth mentioning in this connection that "deuten" means literally "to point to". In this way the broader meaning of interpretation is well shown, namely to draw a person's attention to another meaning of the line of thought or action he is just pursuing. To interpret, therefore, is to transfer or to translate something from one context to another.

Concerning the question of so-called deep interpretations, they have their value in dealing with psychotic cases in particular, but also in certain types of case and in certain phases of nearly all cases of neurotics. I am thinking in particular of patients who tend rather to cling to the everyday surface of things, to indulge in small talk, or

† *The Interpretation of Dreams*

who show an obstinate but completely silent resistance. In such cases, a "deep interpretation" sometimes breaks through the resistance or else makes it more acute and manifest.

With all this occasional value of deep interpretations, it is important to keep in mind as a general principle that interpretations should follow the view laid down by Freud, namely to start always from the surface of things, from that which is manifestly present.

EXAMPLE OF AN INTERPRETATION: THE OLD HOUSE

Mr Ch is a man who had improved in the group in the sense that he had become more secure in his work, more ready to be a boss according to his position and freer all round at home too. Inside the group situation he was still struggling in connection with his withdrawal and thus missing important information. Sometimes, although on rare occasions, he actually fell asleep or nearly so. This has been recognised as a rebellion against his father in that he could not accept anything from him, whereas he felt at the same time that it was also important to listen to him. This disturbance in relation to the group and the conductor was very much in the centre of his conflict inside the group. Now Mr Ch reported that he had repeated dreams recently about the old house. By that he meant the house in which he and his family had lived when he joined the group two years previously. It was a house of an old-fashioned type, similar to the one in which he was brought up. At the time when he moved house this was discussed in the group and related to changes going on in him. His wife hated living in London and wanted to live in the country. Mr Ch obliged and was quite happy to do so. He enjoyed his new abode on a river in the country and everything was nice. He nevertheless dreamt now of *longing* to be in the old house.

At this point Mr H another member of the group said: "Well, it is quite clear what the interpretation is, you must refer to some change going on with you in the group". Mr Ch seemed to accept this interpretation, saying that he had not thought about it himself but he was sure it was correct. There was however still the reference to the old house in the sense of the parental house. Mr Ch had done better than his father in spite of rebelling against the father's standards, who was a civil servant. He was more adventurous than the father. For instance he had recently developed plans to buy a boutique in addition to his job as a journalist. He also said that it had now become easier for him to contemplate having a night out sometimes, although there was no particular woman in his life at the moment. He had shown this tendency repeatedly. At one time he had tried to be intimate with another married woman but found himself impotent. But now the attitude of his wife seemed to have changed slightly. Her attitude had always been that she might understand if he did such things. She might forgive him, but if she knew, things would never be the same again. More recently the wife had started to flirt with another man of which both of them were aware. Mr Ch was ambivalent about this but indicated that it would free him to be a little promiscuous himself. At this point I merely said to him "This would be very different from your father, wouldn't it?" This found an echo in Mr Ch. It became clear that the change of house had sexual connotations too, such as changing wives, his own wife being as it were the old house, and that his being more adventurous than his father also had its double meaning.

The point about this type of interpretation is that I preferred it to spelling out in more detail the relationship between his rebellion against his father in terms of learning at school, in terms of career and the sexual rivalry and liberty at the back of it. It was at this particular level at that moment that the interpretation given had the right depth — it was neither too superficial nor too deep and thus acceptable, had an effect and a mutative quality as far as the patient was concerned. This is a type of interpretation which I frequently apply and prefer.

There is no doubt that interpretations form an essential, useful and important part of our technique, but we should always keep in mind that in giving an interpretation we do the work which the patient ought to do. In case of doubt I therefore prefer the patient to find out for himself. It should be unnecessary to link up interpretation and the acceptance or rejection of interpretations continuously with introjection and projection processes, true as this is, because these are rather metapsychological concepts, to use Freud's term. It's rather as if one were to point out the grammar in the middle of a sentence. If this is done it leads to the patient talking and visualising all the time what is going on, in what are basically oral-regressive terms of intake and output, of accepting and rejecting in the libidinal and destructive sense. It is not sure that only transference interpretations are mutative to use Strachey's happy term. I do not see that deeply mutative changes cannot occur when we analyse or interpret significant meaning in other actual experiences or relationships in or outside the session. This is particularly obvious in a group.

The modern tendency to put transference interpretations totally and explicitly into the centre of the analytic procedure is open to grave doubt. This can be overdone and in fact reinforces the neurosis. It seems to me that the transference phenomenon, though essential for human relationships and for analysis to take place, is nevertheless in a certain sense the victory of the neurosis over both therapist and patient alike. Thus I cannot agree with the monopoly conceded in certain techniques to the transference and its interpretation. Every interpretation has transference implications and for that matter countertransference implications. We must discern these from interpretations directly concerned with transference itself. The mere fact that the therapist responds to material by interpreting it has considerable transference implications; similarly the absence of response on his part, his expectant attitude.

As far as direct transference interpretations are concerned they seem particularly important, firstly, when transferences are making themselves felt as resistance and, secondly, when these transference reactions in themselves are at that moment the most relevant communication. I will again stress that the phenomenon of transference is in itself the most powerful resistance and defence against change. This is true for the negative transference and also perhaps ultimately most of all for the positive transference. It is well known the patient misunderstands his analyst in the role of the person whom he represents. What is less looked upon is that in consequence of this the actual meaning of the analyst's interpretations can be completely distorted, can be neutralised or denied, and thus lose all the therapeutic meaning they were meant to serve.

Before talking of interpretation in group analysis more particularly, I would once more stress the importance of distinguishing interpreting from analysing, which latter activity is far more comprehensive. One might go as far as to say that *interpretation comes in where analysis fails.* Analysing in this sense is the establishment of more and more specific meaning by patient exploration. We certainly take into account the unconscious meaning in symbolic or other language but only insofar as we have evidence for this, in the actual context of the communication.

It is true for all interpretations, whether given in the individual or in the group situation, that they should not be too deep nor too superficial. I will later give some examples, especially of that kind of interpretation which I avoid, as for instance what I call "plunging" interpretations or aggressive interpretations.

INTERPRETATION IN GROUP ANALYSIS

a) On the Part Of The Patients

In the group-analytic group interpretations are going on all the time, consciously and unconsciously. With the *conscious* part we can deal quickly. The analytic group develops, one might say, an interpretative culture, in which to some extent the patients consciously participate. As they become more aware of the usefulness and significance of interpretations they practise them actively. This, to some extent, is a positive and welcome contribution. It can also very easily degenerate into a definite resistance and frequently does so. The paramount idea of such behaviour can be identification with the therapist and in particular competitiveness with him or for him. The most outstanding example is what is known as the *assistant conductor.* The analyst's task in this is of course to analyse this resistance. More important is the *unconscious* process of interpretation in such a group which, in my opinion, is a continuous one. It rests on the fact that all contributions as they follow upon each other are in part associations, in part reactions and responses to what has been going on before..

RESONANCE, SPECIALLY BETWEEN TWO MEN

We will begin with a relatively simple example confined in the main to two interacting people. Mr U began attacking me, the conductor, for having said to him he might sometimes be wrong. In a slightly paranoid fashion he transformed this into an accusation as if I had treated him dangerously and without due respect for his sensitivity. It made him uncertain, not only about interpretations here in the group, but also about everything outside, for example his writing and, in a way, he wanted to hold me responsible. I listened carefully to him, made some remarks, but, on the whole, could leave the matter to other members of the group to deal with. It became quite clear that in his own feeling such remarks can symbolically castrate him, they can put into question the whole security of his being and his confidence that what he produces is valid. He called this a "realisation". Later on Mr U mentioned his concern with human decay. He thought in particular of a play by Beckett. He was very horrified by the thought of decay. This was taken up by Mr L whose first session it was that evening. He spoke at great length. The words with which he took the matter up were 'one can find it in oneself . . . ' . . 'I find it myself in my own person', referring to this decay.

In the course of his talk to the group, U spoke a great deal about his impotence, that he has never been able to penetrate, and further about his whole problem about being half Jewish and the secret that was made about this. In fact his mother was the Jewish parent and the story turned to his circumcision which he underwent later than is usual, and consequently had some trouble with this. Here there is a clear link, an unconscious interpretation as it were, between decay, Jewishness, circumcision and castration. He also mentioned that he was threatened as a child, in the sense that if a child hit his mother he would be killed and buried in such a way that he would be stood upright in his grave with the offending hand sticking out so that it would wither away. The reference here between castration, death and masturbation becomes clear. He had also spoken about the importance of his mother for him and also his reaction to another therapist's remark who had said that he, the patient, identified himself with his mother. This stimulated great apprehension in Mr L that he may be a homosexual because he knew that homosexuals usually identify with their mothers. For him the idea of being "a queer" was the most horrifying one. In this connection, he also mentioned that his mother never tolerated him or his brother really knowing anything. For instance, his brother was a consultant physician, but when he talked about anything medical, the mother pooh-poohed it and devalued it. In short the mother literally castrates him and his brother. In this way Mr L took up U's reaction to me. It can be seen that there was complete unconscious understanding between Mr U and Mr L, in that the one had felt treated by me exactly in the way as Mr L described of his mother, and on the other hand, Mr L had taken up the horror of decay as a key note for entering into his life story. It is also interesting that Mr U had literally penetrated with great aggressiveness in verbal ways into the group as was pointed out to him on this occasion and had in a displaced form denied his castration. He had indeed indulged in a very aggressive and in a sense potent way, whereas in actual life, in physical contact with women, he was not able to do so. He went through all the moves in his behaviour inside the session, (in relation to me as father mostly and to the group as mother), of which in actual life he was afraid as he was of the inside of a woman. On a deeper level, the group symbolised the inside of the woman, ultimately of the mother.

RESONANCE IN THE GROUP
The following example is more difficult to make transparent in a condensed account. It shows the same mechanism of unconscious intercommunication, resonance, by contrast involving practically all the members of the group.

This was a session after an Easter break. The two last sessions before the holiday had been much concerned with death in an obvious reference to the group's reaction to the break. In this first session after the holiday the basic theme was that of dependency. First Miss LA talked of her despair and of her family's reaction, and in particular her mother's reaction against the group. She underlined the conflict between this and her own desperate dependency on the group. This was echoed by Miss BI who also described her dependency conflict with her own mother which in turn was echoed by Mrs MC. Mr U deplored his dependency on Dr F whom he links up with a grandmother and a clergyman. The theme of death was again raised by Mr N who reported a long story of his wife and that she had been worried about the possible death of a new-born child because of its lack of breathing. This evoked Miss BI's remembering about her nightmares and the great difficulty and agony in not being able to breathe, thus almost interpreting her nightmare as a form of birth and separation anxiety. Mr N spoke of his wife's resentment of his own dependency on the group which provoked Mr B to report again how his own wife was against his attendance at and dependency on the group. It looks as if in the example of these two wives and Miss LA's mother respectively the regressive dependency on the group is felt and interpreted also as taking their own motherly place away, as threatening them with losing this dependency, (we would call it fixation) and possibly making them less dependent altogether. Taking into account some interesting differential behaviour between two of the other members my own conclusion after this group was that the fear was stimulated by death wishes against the therapist and fears about losing him and the group. This is where this particular total reaction is closely linked with the transference situation.

b) Unconscious Interpretations on the Part of the Group

In group analysis we consider the contributions of different members as they follow upon each other as having an associative connection (group association). There is frequently an element of unconscious interpretation involved. Sometimes this is more obvious than at other times, but in a sense it is always present. In the following I can only give one brief example which is not typical insofar as only three persons are involved but it will show how deep such interpretations go and how significant they are.

Mr E sits with his shoes completely untied. The co-therapist draws attention to this after some silence. He has no particular answer to her question why he left his shoes untied but Mr M, a relative newcomer to the group who knows little as yet about Mr E says "shoes are in a way like another skin". I will give some of the background of this association or unconscious interpretation. Mr E has a very strong preoccupation with castration and in particular with circumcision. When this patient was a boy he had to have an operation for appendicitis. With the connivance of the father, himself a surgeon, this operation was used at the same time to have the boy circumcised. When he first became aware of this, after the operation, the patient was very much concerned, apart from his pain, and had to be consoled by the nurses. He was for many years completely impotent after this, even as regards masturbation, until he overcame, in a physical way, this impotence with the help of "very friendly nurses". He acts out his impotence in life in protest against his father by being a failure. At the present time he makes strong attempts to be a success and has transferred a great deal of his resentment against his father to the group and more particularly to me. Occasionally his concern about the male organ, his father's organ, breaks through in so many words but as a rule is strongly denied.

For interest's sake, I will add some more of the analysis in this particular respect, also because it forms a good example of what I call a *boundary incident*, that is to say, something that is taking place at the boundary of the therapeutic situation. This same patient Mr E once missed a session and declared next time that he had a dental appointment immediately before the session and his dentist suggested taking out another tooth, using the phrase "while we are about it", and this made him miss the session. The character of a boundary incident is here typically indicated by the encroachment upon the therapeutic session itself. The analysis of this event brought out for the first time the whole story about his appendix operation which was followed by the circumcision when *the same words were used:* "while we are about it". He thus lost his foreskin with all the consequences indicated.

The other patient, who had no knowledge at all of any of this when he said "shoes are like another skin" had unconsciously analysed the meaning of untied shoes as referring to the foreskin. As always there are many more intricate elements entering into this both as regards the individuals concerned as well as the group but we must leave it at that.

ANOTHER SHORT EXAMPLE
In another group X talks about his smothering mother. (X suffers from lifelong impotence). Dr B begins immediately to speak of the need for her to clean her eight year old's behind after his using the toilet as he will always make this necessary, refusing to clean himself. In connection with this she speaks also of the painful cleaning of his foreskin. This theme of a mother's over concern for the intimate functions, especially anal functions, of the child and the consequences is followed further by other members of the group (Dr B's husband is also impotent). It is noteworthy by the way that at the very next session Dr B reported that *her boy had changed* and had not since come to her demanding to be cleaned.

A PATIENT'S "INTERPRETATION"
Here is a situation which concerned the whole group but which was decisively

changed by an enlightening observation coming from one particular patient. Being made explicit by me and others it had the effect of a "switching" interpretation, changing the situation not only for this patient but for the whole group, and allowing a different and new understanding of the problem with which they were concerned.

The theme is simple enough and is a frequent one. It is about the therapist not giving them enough, not giving them the right interpretations and so forth. There is also the implication that the therapist knows the answers. For some unknown reason only will he not let the group have his knowledge or his wisdom. Mr Ch whom we already know personifies and dramatises this situation in relation to the group as well as to the conductor. He withdraws into a kind of trance at times which has often been analysed. It certainly has a lot to do with the attention he wishes to receive from the therapist-father, but which at the same time he feels embarrassed to demand or to accept. This time the members of the group make particularly clear that their parents *knew* the secret but wouldn't give it away, or let them, the children, have access to it. It was pointed out that they referred to their parents' sexual knowledge; the father knowing how to make love to the mother. At this point Mr Ch suddenly remembered how at the age of about eleven he already knew about sex, but insisted nevertheless that his father tell him "the facts of life".

His father was very embarrassed about this. He tried to fulfill the son's demands but did so ineffectually. When this urge to know something which the parents knew but wouldn't tell them was first interpreted, the group grew silent. The newly introduced note of the clumsy and inefficient father was now taken up by Mr NE who when young used to travel home with his father, sometimes after the father had had a few drinks. His father would drop off to sleep in the train and snore "like a pig". The young Mr NE would move to another seat and pretend he did not know his father. This also clearly referred to Ch's description of his parents as being dull and his disowning them. The new note introduced by Mr Ch and taken up by myself was that "knowledge" was *knowledge of the facts of life* in the biblical and sexual sense, shed quite a new light on the whole situation. It was clear now that the group was concerned with the superior rights and knowledge of the two therapists, representing the two parents, and their freedom of sexual grown-up life. The group looked upon this with infantile curiosity and impotence, with ambivalent demand of knowing and refusal to be told. Yet real knowledge *must* come from the parent figure. I, the patient, must not know or I give myself away, but I cannot grow up if I don't know; I must still ask my father to tell me, to give me his knowledge, his sexual power, his sexual secret. But as long as I have to ask my father I get into my own infantile ambivalent conflict.

Looking back on the session M had already put the sexual theme to the group through a dream, but they had displaced it into knowledge about psychology, being given the right interpretation and so forth. Now when the problem became highlighted by personification, and short circuited between one or two patients and the therapist, it became possible for the group to have insight into their real concern.

Communication in a group can be understood on different levels, arising from a central core of a basic universal language. The conscious or unconscious interpretations of which some examples have just been given are as significant for the giver as for the receiver. They all make sense in the common pool of meaning, the network of communication, the matrix of the group. On the fact that meaning refers to different levels at the same time rests the specificity of meaning for each individual. Each individual picks out, as it were, from a common pool that which is most meaningful to him personally. This is a very rough description of what I have termed *resonance*. Theoretically speaking, it rests on the difference in levels of psychosexual development, the regressive levels; it rests on the different reaction formations and ways of defence in which the ego deals with conflicting material. These processes play on a scale from the earliest development to the present day. They comprise super-ego reactions, attitudes or specific inter-reactions of attitudes towards certain stimuli or problems. Meaning is thus always relevant in the context of the whole group in its different configurations, as well as for each participating individual himself.

c) On the Part of the Conductor

The conductor need not necessarily be conscious of this all the time, but he can quite simply find the right note for his interventions or interpretations, if he is receptive and takes things up on the level on which they are presented. We may now concentrate on the selective aspects of interpretation on the part of the conductor as a deliberate form of verbal communication. We have mentioned that the choice as to what to take up and when and in what way is founded upon the conductor's orientation as gained from the processes taking place which have just been indicated. It is my contention that the way in which the conductor arrives at his interpretations is not principally different from that of other members of the group. All we can claim is that the spectrum of his activity should be shifted towards the unconscious or pre-conscious level. As an expert the conductor is in charge of the group and in a significantly different role from the rest. He has many functions and many things to watch which are not our concern here as we wish to make some observations solely on his function as interpreter. He is less involved and therefore is in a better position to act as an interpreter, to judge what are the most important aspects, to have in mind questions of timing and so forth.

The conductor should be able to follow the patients' communications. All behaviour is considered a communication relevant to the therapeutic situation. He should be able to understand these communications especially those on a verbal level as being meaningful in different keys, as it were, on different levels at the same time. In choosing the level of his own communication he is guided by the group's preferred language of the moment. Meaning is understood in terms of the group as a whole as well as of all the individuals composing the group. In my opinion the sharp differentiation between so-called group and so-called individual interpretations is not justified.

Interpretations are always significant for the group as a whole, that is for all the members assembled in the treatment room. They may be addressed to any particular individual or refer to configurations or relationships within the group or between the group and the conductor. Interpretations are not merely concerned with the on-going session but range over the whole history of the group. Whereas interpretations are usually brief and, with me, unobtrusive and almost conversational, there are certain exceptions to this when prolonged statements can occur. The following are some outstanding examples.

    a) summary statements concerning individuals
    b) what I refer to as 'boundary' incidents
    c) when it becomes important to give the group an interpretation of its total behaviour, especially at points of crisis.

In order to be mutative, interpretations must be based on the available experience of the moment and as near as possible to the emotional level which seems to be most active. The dynamic effect is often due to the change of focus from one context to another, quite different, one so that a new meaning emerges.

"T" SITUATION AND THE OUTSTANDING AREAS OF INTERPRETATION

I have proposed that any psychotherapeutic or teaching situation should be clearly defined, with accurate demarcations of its limitations or boundaries. If so defined it might be referred to as a "T" situation (T symbolising treatment, teaching or training and transference). The group-analytic situation has been defined in this way. Assuming its characteristics to be known and observed the following

applies: The outstanding areas to which interpretations usually refer
are —

1) The ongoing interactive group processes;

2) The conflict which the individual repeats in the group situation. This, an expression of repetition compulsion, is the most salient
way in which the individual neurosis can tell in the group;

3) In connection with this, past experience, in particular
childhood experience, which comes to us rather than being looked
for by us;

4) The current experience in life outside the immediate treatment
situation 'inside the plexus', and in connection with this

5) the particularly important area of the boundary incidents
between ongoing group (1) and ongoing life (4).

All these areas are approached in the light of the ongoing dynamic
situation in the group. The reality situation in which the patients and
the therapist find themselves must always be respected and taken
into account when analysing and interpreting.

Interpretation is only one of the analyst's functions. It is a slow
process which goes on continuously and which culminates only from
time to time in the actual act of making an interpretation in the
usual sense of the term. It seems important not to add new elements
without sufficient evidence but to develop slowly, from his own
communications, a new interpretation of what the patient is, says or
does. These communications are originally disconnected through
being expressed on different levels of language as it were; one might
say in different keys in the musical sense. They are also separated in
time by being dispersed over different sessions. Using our psychoanalytic experience to the full we must be guided continuously by
the patient's own clues and must avoid forcing our own schemata
upon his.

Interpretations are brought out in the light of activated experience
and in the fire of the presenting emotion. In my usage, the 'here and
now' is understood in terms of the total situation, not merely the
patient-therapist relationship. It includes current reality, current
experience and the current network. There is no active search for the
past, but it comes dynamically into the situation and is then
considered as important and fully accepted as part of the ongoing
analysis.

I do not pull transference upon my own person more than is
necessary, but refer these reactions to the group as a whole. Whereas

in my own mind I interpret all the time, I am economic in the use of verbal interpretations. I do not wish to enhance my own importance in the group nor to cultivate and feed the hunger for dependency. My inner work tells perhaps in the nature and the timing of my interpretations and other interventions and in the total management of the group.

The guiding lines for interpreting on the part of the therapist may be stated as follows: Interpretation is called for when there is a blockage in communication. It will be particularly concerned with resistances, including transference. Its form and content should be determined by the ongoing interaction and communication as experienced by the group. For its location and timing the emotion of the patients should be followed.

1) I will give here some brief examples of such interpretations as I usually *avoid*.

A. "Plunging" interpretations. They are usually combined with what appear to me premature and uncalled for incursions into transference reactions. I will use some examples from psychoanalytical communications which are now many years old. I am using these examples because they have the advantage of often giving literal details of the actual interpretations. I can of course quote only very condensed versions.

a) The masturbation theme was topical. The patient had admitted with great shame that she masturbated. She now appeared one day with scarlet nail varnish and spent the early part of the session tearing a piece of paper into smaller and smaller pieces. This was accompanied by associations concerning her revulsion of having been breast-fed (one can assume that this association is already induced by the analyst's attitude). "I interpreted to her how she felt the breast was revolting because she felt she had torn it to bits with her nails which were stained with blood. She asked me not to say things like that as they terrified her and I interpreted that she felt terrified of this torn breast, which she felt as an internal persecutor of which I was the representative when I made these interpretations to her."

b) The patient reports that when he was about sixteen years old their house had been burgled. He had had an intuitive feeling that something like this might happen and had rung his home number. When he got home he found his house had in fact been burgled. He thought he must have disturbed the burglars through telephoning because they had been through his own and his sister's room and had been halfway through his parents' room when they broke off. The idea that he had interrupted the burglars made him feel omnipotent. After this he made his father put bars on all the windows and was so frightened that for two weeks he slept in the parents' bedroom. I interpreted: "the burglar whom you felt you must keep out is the bad father breaking in to have intercourse with mother, you feel that he will come and kill you, for omnipotently and from a distance disturbing them in their room. Later you actually sleep in their room to make sure they don't have intercourse." And the analyst adds: "The fact that he told me that after this event he slept in his parents' bedroom made me feel that the burglar was representing a bad father whom he wanted to keep out of his mother. But I think that the burglar must also have represented a bad part of himself breaking in on his parents." The patient now says that the analyst's interpretations go into him like a ray of light but inside they become diffused, broken up and turned into faeces. Then he altered it and said "no, into semen and I keep it inside me".

The analyst reports: "I said that the interpretations which I put into you, you attack, break up, turn into faeces and then into semen. But I think you do not use the interpretations to make a good baby, you steal it and keep it for yourself as semen." Not surprisingly the report continues: "there followed a period in which some material was very disjointed and the patient himself commented on this fact."

The patient then recalls the fact that he has disliked the idea of his mother coming over to England. I interpreted: "You felt no shame with them afterwards because the part of yourself which you felt was crazy and linked with faeces was split off. When mother, who is felt to have the madness in her, suggests coming over to England, and again last night when the cat jumped on you, you felt that the mad anal part of yourself was getting back at you and you screamed."

I would call these interpretations *plunging*, even if they are correct. In the context quoted, I would doubt their validity and feel that they contain at least as much of the analyst's as of the patient's phantasy.

Another example:

c) Mrs S described how much better she was feeling generally. She recalled a tummy upset that morning which made her wonder if she would be able to come. Even as she thought this she found herself preparing for the journey. Because the conductor and driver were talking, the bus was late starting, and she thought she was bound to be late. "Then suddenly it flashed through her mind that I knew that I could be physically attracted or repulsed by men, and I knew I wanted a sexual side to my life." The analyst interpreted that Mrs S felt that she had eaten up the penis, that it was bound to attack her inside, or that having experienced loving feelings towards the analyst as father, she would then feel repulsed as if the analyst had become maimed in the relationship. Then the bus would be late and so would she. In other words the bus would have lost out and she by identification would be similarly impeded.

I have deliberately used examples at random to show that these are not individual peculiarities, although in this form they are perhaps characteristic of a certain minority type of English psychoanalyst. One can often clearly see the aggressive note in the analyst, or his paranoid or narcissistic make-up, his depression, and so on.

Other types of interpretation to be avoided:

B. One often finds, especially in beginners, a tendency to *catch out* the patient for instance by confronting him with contradictions such as "and yet you have said your father was so and so . ." or ". . but last time you told us quite the contrary, that your mother was very kind to you . ."

C. *Linking interpretations,* that is to say when the analyst makes connections for the patients, doing their thinking for them. These are specially popular amongst analysts who are somewhat insecure, who feel the need to justify their existence, and are pleased when they can show their analytic functions to the group. Such interpretations are mostly harmless, but are neither useful nor helpful, especially not in the form of transference interpretations. They have the effect of drawing away from the immediate here and now of the transference.

D. As a last category in this list of interpretations to be avoided, I will mention those interpretations which tend to be *classifying* or *categorising* instead of staying with the actual concrete experience as it is manifest in the patients' contribution. This is an important consideration but here I can only hint at what is meant. For instance, a patient whose main symptom was impotence spoke of how he was afraid to be made ridiculous in the group, how he might feel small, how in fact he did feel small and couldn't grow up; after some thought he added "don't want to grow up". Or, a man whose firm was amalgamating with another described his enormous concern as to how he would be placed in seniority and otherwise amongst the new partners. He reanimated his deep conviction that it would be discovered that he was not really entitled to be in such a good position.

In both these cases a co-conductor brought in the concept of "castration". Now this was undoubtedly correct but was ill-timed and unhelpful in that the actual castration fear was expressed much more vividly — emotionally and experientially — in what the patient actually said. One must remember here that the manifest communication contains in it not only the early experience but often the particularly important *specific* meaning in which the anxiety occurs.

2) *Transference interpretations* Patients frequently present their transference behaviour first in relation to the therapist or in relation to each other. It is especially instructive for them to experience its immediate meaning in the group and in current life and then to discover by themselves the very important links to past parental or sibling relationships. It is my experience that the clear recognition of

the historical Transference significance often follows change, rather than anteceding it. Individuals sometimes also transfer clearly to the group as a whole. In my opinion this, like everything else, must also be seen on different levels. On a very deep, archaic level, as I have said before, the group represents the mother. On other levels it represents all sorts of things at different times and for different patients, very often a kind of super-ego, a critical and feared authority. It has become clear to me, especially in recent years, that this repetition is the way in which the individual Transference neurosis establishes itself in the group situation. It is a regular occurrence and always contains the key to the very basic and *individual* side of the patient's neurosis, in an exact parallel to the Transference neurosis in a two-personal situation in psychoanalysis. Following Freud, I would be inclined to describe this more adequately as repetition-compulsion.

Coming now to the transference interpretations (with a small t) in the wider and broader sense, these are of course legion and occupy us all the time. Nevertheless, in my own approach, they do not monopolise my, or the group's central interest. We look upon them in the bigger framework of the treatment (T) situation which, as I have mentioned, comprises not only the immediate session but occurrences in daily life and boundary incidents.

In the following example, the transference reaction in that wider sense concerns the group as a whole.

The group in one particular session cut me out completely. Had I not said anything at all during this session I think they would have taken no notice of me. As it was, I pointed out their behaviour after about one hour of the session, and how it affected me. Various communications confirmed my interpretation, especially also why nobody had looked at me or why at the beginning they had not taken any notice when I entered the room. In the following session the group spent a long time talking of death and in particular parental death, their horror of death and dead bodies and dying people and so forth. It became clear that the last time they had "silenced" me, in a sense killed me. This was not only an expression of their aggression towards me but also of their phobic fear for me and they had suffered a great deal from the fact that I had not joined in, had not shown any signs of life. This time they were not cutting me out or dead, but were falling over each other with communications at such speed and intensity that I had to be very active to make myself heard when I wanted to make a contribution. Then I was listened to with respect. (We shall come back to this topic when discussing interpretations given to the group as a whole, total group interpretations.)

Interpretations, especially "transference" interpretation as a defence

A certain type of *linking* interpretation may be considered here from the aspect of unconscious countertransference meaning, of drawing away from the here and now.

Once Miss PA, a schizoid girl, was very closely concerned with not knowing what was in my head and I was hoping to get to grips with some deep-going confusion in her identity when my co-conductress intervened and said "Isn't that the same feeling as you have with your mother?" and thus gave the patient a good alibi to talk about her mother.

In another example, the co-conductor herself was the focus of intense feeling on the part of Mrs A. She at once said to her "Isn't that the same thing you do to your mother?" or "is that why you also do not like to be touched by your mother?"

ANALYSING

We have had to say quite a bit about interpretation. I wish, therefore, once more to emphasise that interpretation in a more precise sense is only one, if an important one, of the activities of the group analyst. His total activity is analysing. This in turn can be taken in a more exact as well as in a wider sense in which it corresponds to the total process of establishing and maintaining the group-analytic situation and of the translation of meaning from a less conscious form of communication to a conscious verbal one. We have already spoken about these activities and illustrated them by examples.

In this type of therapeutic group, the development of the individual is our ultimate aim. There is no question of aiming at conformity or toeing the line. Even what is normal or not is a question of values which might be shared or not and which should indeed be critically considered even though these values may be generally accepted by the group. The creative nature of the conductor's task has been mentioned. It is important for the therapist to admit that his personal influence is inevitably strong, in spite of all his precautions to minimise this. He then should use it consciously rather than haphazardly or unconsciously, helping the patients to become what they are. The importance of his basic modesty must be stressed as otherwise the temptation for him to feel omnipotent is great. This in turn has to do with his ethical integrity. For this reason alone, if not for many others, the conductor cannot participate in the same way as other group members do. He ought to bring his own involvements into the open wherever the process of communication makes this desirable. However he need not bring his own personal countertransference reactions into the procedure except when they involve the group and he cannot for some reason deal with them sufficiently by himself alone. In some situations, the best way to deal with these personal reactions, even from the conductor's own point of view, is the open discussion with the group members.

ORIENTATION

We have now to say more about the group analyst's orientation in this complicated process on which all his interventions must depend. We have pointed out that the interacting psychological processes are seen as taking place in the group matrix while at the same time involving the various individuals in different specific ways and constellations. Just as the individual's mind is a complex of inter-acting processes (personal matrix), mental processes interact in the concert of the group (group matrix). These processes relate to each other in manifold ways and on a variety of different levels. The group-analytic group has been termed a psyche group. We are altogether concerned with psychological processes. Whereas the conductor has to look upon and expose himself to the total of these interacting processes, the members are concerned only with what they themselves experience, feel, observe, what they wish to express by action, or desire and ultimately try to say in words without reservation and/or to voice their reservations also. The conductor by contrast has to observe what goes on altogether, including himself, although it is only exceptionally necessary for him to communicate his own personal experiences, his private experiences as it were, when the interest of the group demands this. Whereas the members use the group for their own interest, the conductor alone puts the group's interest first and foremost. He is in the service of the group. In this way, the conductor's function is complementary to that of the other members. All events, all observable phenomena are treated as communications whose meaning should become understood and shareable.

There are a variety of configurations as to what is expressed, by whom and to whom. For instance, one member may speak to another or others. Some of them may turn to one, or to a number of others. Any of this may be addressed to the conductor in particular.

Indeed the whole group may address him. The conductor on his part uses the same varieties of communication. All this is the foreground, the figure of a process which in its totality comprises the whole group and on the ground of which meaning becomes defined, interpretation springs to life. It must be hoped that the reference here to the *Gestalt* idea of figure and ground as inseparable is understood; similarly, the fact that one can switch, so that what was ground becomes figure or foreground and what was figure recedes into the background. In my own opinion this is not merely a way of perception but it corresponds to the actual ongoing psychodynamics in the group situation. I believe that Wolfgang Köhler has put forward similar views.

LOCATION

The conductor's first task is not merely to perceive meaning, but also to place it in the appropriate dynamic setting. I have termed this process *location*. This process of location can best be understood on the basis of *Gestalt* theory in the sense just indicated. Location presupposes the conductor becoming aware of the relevant configuration of the observable phenomena. Thus he can divine the relevant key in which the group speaks at that moment. Only in speaking back to the group in that same key can he hope to be understood relatively well. A simpler way of putting this is that the good conductor, the good therapist, talks back in the language in which things reach him, in the language current amongst the members of the group.

Different interpretations are not contradictory but correspond to particular perspectives, similar to objects being photographed from different points. This location is particularly important when it refers to a *disturbance* in communication, to resistances or defences which prevent a free flow of communications or their reception and thus the sharing of them. We must accept that the language of these interactions is not confined to words, but extends to inflexions of voice; manner of speaking, looking, to expressions, gestures; actions or, in view of their restrictions, intended actions; emotional reactions of all sorts — sympathy, condemnation or contempt, attraction or disgust, love, hatred and indifference.

These primary levels correspond to the *foundation* matrix, based on the biological properties of the species, but also on the culturally firmly embedded values and reactions. These have been developed and transmitted, especially in the nuclear family, in the social network, class, etc. and have been maintained or modified by the intimate plexus in which the person now moves.

All this is now temporarily replaced by the artificially created, strange but potentially very intimate group network in the "T" situation, more intimate than any other encounter type of therapeutic group. This *dynamic* matrix is in fact the theatre of operation of ongoing change.

RESONANCE

All participants speak and understand this language, interpret or misinterpret it significantly, each according to his particular "resonance", corresponding to his own psychopathology or his special reaction to the person or to the inference implied at this moment in time. This communicational transaction is instinctive and is regressively activated on different libidinal and aggressive levels at one and the same time, mobilising early ego and super-ego developmental stages as well as corresponding defences and reaction-formations. Transference and repetition-compulsion enter into this primary process, this psychotic-like world of experience and expression, and bring primordial and infantile experience alive into the context of the ongoing therapeutic (T) situation.

The conductor must know this language. He should have learned it from his own experience and that of others and must continue to use it, a never-ending process of learning. He should be ahead of his patients in this, should hear the "voice of the symbol" as M. Grotjahn has recently termed it.† Then he must patiently wait for them to catch up, cautiously helping here and there perhaps, but most concerned with what is in the way, blocking the group's own understanding.

He should always test whether this bloc is not in himself, whether the impediment does not include him, or even emanate from himself. The conductor must always be ready to assume that the group tries to tell him more than he understands, or something different, something else.

†Martin Grotjahn *The Voice of the Symbol* Los Angeles, Mara Books, 1971.

For a more precise understanding of the concepts touched upon here, I must again refer the reader to a theoretical account, but what has been said should at least give an idea of the framework in which the group conductor operates. With this in mind, we can appreciate some of his own operations in more detail.

THE ANALYTICAL ATTITUDE

Having spoken of the analytical attitude of the conductor, I will attempt, very briefly, to sum up the main points which this implies.

1) That he is receiving all communications, that he is non-directive, clarifying, interpretative; using predominantly verbal means leading eventually to insight.

2) That the relationship which members of the group form to him and to each other is itself made the object of communication and of analysis.

3) That he is non-manipulative in the relationship, as he under-stands his position as a transference figure. He treats the interpersonal relationships in the spirit of a transference situation, even when Transference aspects in the strict sense of the term are not significant.

It is this analytical attitude which enables the group-analytic conductor to deal correctly with transference reactions themselves and with all other events which happen in the same spirit. I prefer not to call all these reactions *transference* but if doing so to spell the noun at least with a small "t" by distinction to *Transference* in the more correct sense, to be spelt with a capital T.

This analytic attitude promotes ever increasing understanding and correspondingly tolerance and by itself alone furthers the freer development of the individual.

PART III

OBSERVATIONS AND MAXIMS

On the whole, the therapist's real contribution can best be defined if we look at the difference between the group left to itself in contrast to the group with himself included.

We shall now give a number of further examples to illustrate the conductor in action in various group situations. They will I hope show much of what has been discussed and also throw some light on conducting in a number of ways which cannot always be systematically presented. The material selected emphasises a variety of situations which may at the same time serve as illustrations for a number of the mechanisms discussed.

BOUNDARY INCIDENTS

In the section on interpretations by the group on an unconscious level an example has already been given of a boundary incident, namely of a patient whose dental appointment was extended and how the taking up and analysing of this incident led straight to one of his most important deep neurotic anxieties.

In order to make clear what is meant by the boundary of the therapeutic situation, here are a few remarks. To my mind the T situation comprises a precisely defined psychological space which is not confined to the consulting room; still less is it in the group therapeutic situation confined to the relationship of the patient to the therapist in particular. Anything that comes to our knowledge belongs to the therapeutic situation, whether the event takes place in the consulting room or elsewhere. In my experience all such events are extremely important and I do not see them, as they have sometimes been defined, as belonging to an *inside-outside* polarity. To me they are inside. They are, however, quite frequently split off by the group and made by them into contrasting "inside" and "outside" events. As for instance when some members mentioned how much better they were, outside in life, and that the difficulties were here, inside the group session. However, in every well defined therapeutic situation, the therapist is clear how far he extends the boundaries of the T situation on his own part, how far he himself goes in his contact with the patient. Though this is not defined in theoretical terms to the group, the group of patients know and find out by trial and experiment where the boundaries lie. It is by experience and behaviour that this is agreed.

Having agreed on this and the group knowing full well where the boundaries are, I now come to events which are taking place exactly on these boundaries. They infringe or impinge from the outside of the defined area of psychological space into the inside of it. For simplicity's sake, we may for the moment envisage the boundaries of the treatment situation to be the same as those of a conventional therapeutic setting, in particular an analytic one. It is true for my previous example, as for the present one now to be reported, that the infringement upon the psychological boundary is expressed by a violation of the boundary of the concrete therapeutic situation: missing a session.

Miss LA had missed one session and had left a message to that effect. When she appeared next time in the group she started off by telling the story of why she had missed last time. What happened was this: she had *a slipped disc in her back*, a thing which she now often gets when she bends in a certain way. Her first telephone call was because she had wanted to come to the group and she hoped that I would know someone who would put her back right in time for the Monday session (her own doctor could not see her until Tuesday). She could not possibly come in the condition in which she found herself, with her back. Only after having failed to reach me, or for that matter for this message to have reached me, had she 'phoned a second time to say she could not attend. She then went to her usual doctor who put her back right by manipulation. The patient had thus already indicated that her back injury belonged here and that she *wanted me to put her back straight* or to be the agent of putting her back straight. She brought out her anger about her affliction: why did she have to have this as well as having to come to the group? She always says "it is a terrible thing to have to come here". It was to her a similar situation as the one in childhood when she was left by her parents in a hospital in a foreign country and felt abandoned. She then brought out another thing. Some time ago she had attacked Mrs MC very strongly as a mother. She now said "It isn't fair to Mrs MC — she isn't my mother." In fact she had said three sessions previously to Mrs MC "I know what she wants but I won't give it to her!" Up to this point the participation of Miss LA had been minimal and in the session prior to this she had not said a word. Now she was participating much more, not only more often, but with much more voice, much more effect, much more in touch with what was going on. Even when she retreats now and withdraws it is not in the same way as before.

Further analysis brought out the following. She could not show feelings strongly to people with whom she was not emotionally involved, as she was for example with her family or her boyfriend. It is therefore quite clear that she was afraid of the breakthrough of emotional involvement in transference. In a sense it is true to say in her case that the people in the group, representing inner figures, inner images, were even more closely related to her than her actual relatives. Some time after this, this patient reported a complete change in her relationship with her actual mother. It was for the first time in her life that she could speak to her mother and she felt her mother had changed so much towards her and spoke in a very different way to her than ever before.

This example illustrates well the profound meaning that such boundary incidents have. One has to be very alert to this important zone of treatment. It is just on the borderline of what patients consider as belonging to the treatment and what they consider to be outside. They give us slight indications, sometimes it may be just someone coming late under special circumstances and then mentioning that such and such has happened. Of course there are very special reasons why certain patients express their salient conflicts in such borderline fashion more often than others. There are also special reasons, in my opinion, and typical reasons at that, why Miss BA had to convert her conflict in this case into an *organic* form, but to go into this would exceed our present purpose.

The extension of the T situation here indicated includes the phenomena known in psychoanalysis as "acting out" but it is more comprehensive than this.

INTERACTIONS ACROSS THE BOUNDARY

I have drawn attention to the importance of watching the area to which I refer as the *boundary* of the therapeutic situation. In the following examples, it will be shown that comparatively harmless "boundary incidents", as for instance giving each other lifts after the session, or having lunch together are significant.

External relationships are often closely related to their own attitude to the therapist or to similar incidents in the group quite unknown to the patients. There are always clear manifest signals and signs of this which are convincing. Positive analysis sometimes succeeds in breaking through this vicious circle.

By positive analysis is meant that these links are actively taken up by the therapist and investigated. This is a point both of some considerable theoretical and definite technical importance. It is not enough for instance to point out to a woman who has fallen in love with a person outside that the therapist has certain similarities with this man. It may be better to point out a very small detail mentioned, such as say, that the same words were used on certain occasions to either, or a remark was made which clearly refers to the therapist or for that matter to some other member of the group and that this was also used towards the person outside.

We had better look at some examples which should be seen as showing both the significance of outside contact between members and the significance of what is happening outside with other people in the patient's life.

Here is the first instance.

The question of outside contact was raised. I gave some advice about the general precautions to be considered, but in this particular case, sanctioned the fact that some patients gave each other lifts after the session. It was emphasised that no rules or laws are imposed but that it is rather a matter of experience which speaks in favour of avoiding outside contact as far as possible. This was met by a certain opposition from S and in a more intellectualised form from Mrs A. They now disclosed that in certain outside contacts they discussed matters which were of importance and which they had not brought up for discussion in the group. An interesting point in connection with this is that S, a very intelligent and alert psychiatrist, almost claimed amnesia of this particular even.. He had shown a strong tendency to minimise Mrs A's influence and generally defended her.

This gave an opportunity to point out S's general tendency to create dividing lines between "deep going experiences outside" as for instance with his girl friend, and the group. This tendency was significant for him and he seemed to recognise it. How significant such current events and relationships are, may be seen from the fact that this man later on married his girl, following her pregnancy and this marriage will certainly influence his whole future life. At the time it was obviously a kind of solution of a conflict with his mother. It was also linked with the treatment situation by "financial" difficulties which he made. This touches on the technical point which was mentioned earlier of the importance of handling financial questions correctly. In this case it may well be that my conceding a modification of fees was not necessarily a good step. Actually now, many years after this, it can be said as far as my knowledge goes that his marriage is happy and as satisfactory as can reasonably be expected.

Mrs A then talked about his (S's) relationship with his mother. He was about to leave his mother — this was true in the geographical sense and was the reason for his feeling financially more embarrassed. It was true in a deeper sense as became clear from the relationship which evolved with his girl friend. As was mentioned he linked this up with his having to pay for his own accommodation when he left his mother and asked for a reduction of fees which was agreed upon. This had happened just a week before the present session. On a previous occasion when he wanted to leave the group significant changes also occurred with another girl friend. These changes he now said he could not remember, although he had then also given financial difficulties as the reason why he intended to leave the group. The conflict was displayed both inside the group and in current life, but the tendency was to use an intermediate situation as compromise. He acted out in the real situation and thus at the same time tried to withhold this from analysis in the group, yet tenuously making clear the inner link with the goings on in the group. In concrete terms Mrs A was a mother figure with whom he could talk. She was at the same time a member of the group and he talked to her, to the mother alone as it were, instead of to the group and me. When in the session just mentioned Mrs A brought this incident back to the group, Mr S claimed amnesia and also expressed his apprehension by defending Mrs A as if she was not responsible for this kind of "sinful" behaviour. At the same time he lived out, rather than acting out, his conflict with his real mother as Mrs A pointed out to him. The girl friend also represented a link, which at the time was insufficiently understood, between all this and his wish to leave the group, or to be thrown out of the group, because he could not pay, or alternatively to achieve special consideration from myself.

In the following example, Miss MG had some outside contact with another member of the group, Mr P. He had been giving her lifts sometimes in his car and they also had lunch together. This relationship had been clear also by their link in various ways within the group itself. Perhaps the following will illustrate how significant this acting out (meeting outside) really was. When P left for Scotland in connection with preparations for his intended marriage, Miss G confessed that she felt personally concerned about his absence. She talked about him and remarked that this was a characteristic feature which she herself felt to be treacherous, or the equivalent of talking behind people's backs. It was understood that her particular involvement was due to a triangular situation in which she herself was involved at the time – involved with a married man who was not marriageable. This also linked up with her marked need to care for lame ducks. In a sense Mr P could be described in those terms. This particular patient, Miss G, had a whole sequence of involvements during her membership of this particular therapeutic group. These relationships literally moved on a scale from unfortunate relationships which were by their very nature one-sided and impossible to implement – the patient quite healthily wanted to marry and have children. Ultimately she made a relationship which one had every reason to envisage as a very good solution for her and her intention to marry. The particular man did not have any of the attributes of a lame duck any more. It is true that he had been married before but his marriage had practically come to an end already quite a number of years prior to his knowing Miss G. Now to the other side.

P's own behaviour was also characteristic for him. Not only had he met and invited Miss G for lunch repeatedly without reporting it readily to the group. He had quite frequently acted out in similar ways with other members of this group in turn. Some of them were doctors or psychiatrists and he managed to consult them in turn outside the group. The psychological background of his marriage reflected the special difficulties he had with women. It was however a very definite solution of his problem and produced quite fundamental changes in him. Originally he had come from overseas and settled in this country under conflict which had to do with an attempt to leave his mother. His then fiancée still had features of his mother or rather perhaps he had managed to provoke her to react in a similar way to him as his mother had done. He also, by the way, saw the group itself as his mother. His situation when engaged provoked a triangular situation and he went rather far with it in his fantasy.

One can see clearly in this example the deep involvement over fundamental problems between the two and the tendency and risk of short-circuiting by these apparently harmless meetings outside the group situation. In fact they stayed harmless in the sense that no intimate life situation, sexual situation and the like, developed. Technically it may well be that this was prevented only by the timely interpretation in the group of these meetings and the special attention given to these type of intimate interactions outside the group. In these examples, elements of 'acting out' are undoubtedly present, though it is more a "living out". The point of special interest seems to me to be that they transgress the T situation, but at the same time register in symbolic language at its very boundary, presenting themselves to successful analysis, if recognised.

INTERPRETATION TO THE GROUP-AS-A-WHOLE

Now here is an example of *two consecutive* sessions in which the conductor makes a deliberate approach to the problem of the group-as-a-whole, as interpreted by him.

In Session 1 there was a sticky, depressed, angry atmosphere, also a number of silences, very unusual for this group. Only one member, Miss A, who is normally reluctant to speak, especially at the beginning of the session, makes a spontaneous contribution. Mr H is by contrast today depressed and does not want to speak. *All* members with the exception of Miss I have *outside* sexual developments with *complications*, otherwise socially they are very much better. For instance Miss A is very much preoccupied with a man; there is a typical anxiety situation reflecting her guilt feelings in relation to her mother — she is much concerned with the other woman. Mrs H has conflict with her husband and there is a fight on. Mr O says he must break with his girl friend. He feels angry, and arrives with the idea of not wanting to talk and reveals his fear of being ridiculed. He himself has recently overcome his impotence and is much concerned with the other man. Had his girl friend had intercourse or not with him? Mr C tells of a revelation of his wife's infidelity but she (the wife) makes light of this and declares him (her husband) to be very much more satisfactory as a man. Mr C's reaction to this is of a peculiar unconcern, a defence which he also uses otherwise. Miss I is chronically afraid that her total incompetence might be revealed in the group. She refers to the four silent members and the silence is now interpreted as doing a "C" on Mr C. Mr L too had a row with his wife, he says he cannot draw enough sexual interest from her but anger is better than nothing. As to the session today he feels peace and quiet in the group. Miss M feels fine outside but bad in the group — she always reflects the mood of the group and its unconscious currents in her own person. The whole group today behaves in the style she, Miss M, usually does. Miss I is triumphant — she feels justified for her usual reaction that the group *is* hostile and unsafe, it never gives one anything, she feels, it is disintegrating and she talks of leaving. She attacks the conductor vehemently, is convinced that he dislikes her though he had helped her a lot in the past.

In Session 2 Miss I is somewhat late. Mrs H tells of difficulties she had on holiday with her husband — that he claims, based on his own dependence, that she should leave her work which is amateurish and in addition she can be sacked. This was too much for her — she has at the same time a violent reaction to L and his attitude towards his own wife — especially as he feels that there is a masculine/feminine conflict in her which is shared by the conductor. When Miss I arrives the conductor takes matters up with her from last time. He admits his own anger. She seems to react well to this.

He now brings in Miss M's problem. Miss M cries silently. Now Miss I is actively participating. As the group was not able to do so, the conductor approached Miss M in connection with her depression which has now also returned outside the group. He points out how she projects all bad feelings into the group. She feels that it makes no difference to speak, that she is afraid of exposure and that she is found worthless — a mess.

Miss A now talks of her progress, seeing how she debased herself with this worthless man. The rest of the time is mainly taken up by Mrs H's hysterical responses and her denial of all sexual meaning. O was absent from this session but this was anticipated and had a longstanding reason.

The understanding of the meaning of the situation is that an inner sexual conflict was dramatised quite generally. They were clearly oedipal transgressions — exposure of them, condemnation by the group as a retaliation on the part of the super-ego, in part clearly in the sense of a castration as projected onto the group. The conductor does not in this case draw hostility onto his own person, but allows the transference to be borne by the group.

These two consecutive sessions are seen as an interacting sequence, the second, by a deliberate plan on the part of the therapist, a response to the first. In both sessions there were significant movements, particular emphasis on those of a triangular sexual nature, as reported, outside the group. Inside the group hostility towards the group as a whole and towards the members of the group separately produced anger, silences and unwillingness to talk and to expose themselves. The group itself became increasingly identified as a fearful, punitive overpowering super-ego, a very definite shift from the previous tendency to make the therapist into a dreaded super-ego figure.

In the first session, there was a three way exchange between Miss A, Mr O and Mr C — again with emphasis on the sexual movement outside the group. Inside the group a general feeling of non-involvement, withdrawal, even a determination not to participate. Interpretation of this led to expressions of anger, overt and subtle which became focussed on the group as a whole, as an entity separate from its members. Things were experienced as being much better outside the group than inside. An interpretation directed towards Miss I resulted in her experiencing this as an attack and she attacked in turn.

In the second session the conductor actively returned to the situation with Miss I which led to strong focussing on anger and passionate destructiveness. The theme of projecting bad feelings into the group as a group emerged, they felt unsafe in the group, embarrassed, unable to talk. The split between inside and outside the sessions continued, along with silences, blocking out and the production of more material associated with triangular sexual situations outside the group.

A further session was lively and productive. The effect was, or turned out to be, as the conductor would have anticipated and wished it to be. If we take in the next group session it can be said that both Miss I and Miss M changed very positively back to a productive way of communication. That day Mrs H was not present as she was on a two week holiday and Mr L was absent owing to a long-term obligation. This had been anticipated for several months and he was obliged to miss this session. In this third session we were a very small group as Mr C had sent a message that he had gone on holiday to Ireland. This was actually not very surprising as the time was just around Easter. The result was that in the third session, the most disturbing agents, the most frightening ones for the others as it turned out, were absent and the rest could ventilate a good deal in connection with this. We cannot however go into further details of this third session in this context.

We may ask more generally what happens as a result of the group's being smaller than its usual composition, when people are missing. Intense negative feelings which have been experienced against other members but which have not found expression are ventilated in the absence of these members, and it is of course of importance to bring this up again when the others are present. The smaller group also appears to produce two other phenomena:

1) the therapist's activities become intensified — as if to make up for the missing members

2) there is a change in the pattern of communication; in the example above, on the part of Miss A. Generally she talked either at the very beginning of the session or not at all. In this smaller group she was active several times during the session, whilst not needing to be the first to talk.

The intensified activity of the therapist and co-therapist was a notable feature in this group. Significant progress was made with several members of the group, particularly in the recognition of feelings of anger and hostility towards certain absent members. The theme of anger and destructive fantasies had been a threat during several preceding sessions. In this session these feelings were acknowledged as being directed towards certain of the absent members, essentially on a transference basis. The question arises, would these feelings have been uncovered without these absences? Would the transference relationships have been illuminated if the previously inhibiting group members involved had been present in this session? I believe the answer is yes, but probably not at this moment. The selective quality of the absent members seemed striking, but nevertheless coincidental.

UNEXPECTED EFFECT OF A STATEMENT MADE BY THE CONDUCTOR

In a previous session there had been some, one or two, newcomers, and I had made a remark that two or three years ought to be enough for anybody. This seems to have raised anxieties of losing the group, of being thrown out, in some the idea had sunk in "Where do we go from here?" The idea of leaving the group and being independent and the true nature of this problem was perhaps best illustrated by Miss A. She reported that she had just these experiences at home and cried saying that her mother said "this group is a luxury, give that up". All this is mixed up with her losing her job, and telling her mother that she wants to be independent, she would like to drive a car. But she does not really think she can do this or really wishes to be independent. Mrs H had opened the session saying she had made a great step forward. She talked about her husband's jealousy of her coming to this group and his concern over money. She compared this with her own father who she felt did not want her to exist, for instance he had minded the money for her music lessons. This was taken up deeply by the group and there was a lot of oedipal material or at least material thus interpreted clearly connected with the problem of dependence/independence in coming here and having to pay for it and also regarding dependency on parents at the present time. The feeling of losing the group was connected in a transference sense with parental demands for independence and parental ruthlessness and refusal to be further materially supporting. This clearly reflected the feeling towards the group and the conductor in the therapeutic situation. It also shows the repercussions in the intimate family network, the plexus, of the patients. Now a dream was told by Miss B which can be well understood as resonance. In the dream Miss B had an experience of helplessness against men. She was totally passive -- at the same time the windows were open. She connected this with not being able to say no to her father, and also with her experience that she can be friends and have intimate relations with men as long as they are committed elsewhere. If some man who is interested in her is not so committed, as it happens at the present time, she then has great hesitations to be sexual and thus to be committed herself. Again she had the experience that she could not speak over the telephone, she could not really say what she felt. This was in various ways linked with other events in the group and I was drawing her attention to what appeared perhaps the deepest level of all in this — namely her fighting against the desire to be absolutely helpless and dependent in relation to her father.

These are just a few examples to show characteristically how they were produced by the group situation which was created by my reminding them that the group is not an institution to depend on for ever. Our attitude as conductors is to give our patients more freedom to develop and to help them to take their lives into their own hands. This raises deep conflict and characteristically brings up the early family situation, oedipal situation, and that they are really afraid to become independent, a kind of fear of freedom. They cling to this dependency in the group which thus has a more profound meaning.

It appears to me interesting that all this was triggered off not by an interpretation but by a serious pronouncement in the role of the expert, the authority, in the sense "you ought really to think of coming to an end with this one day and even before too long".

In connection with this there was one specific element worth noting, which was especially stressed by Mrs H and Miss O. What they felt was that their particular kind of helplessness rooted in the neurotic provocation of their partner, and they were annoyed when Dr N doubted the fact that the other person concerned was important and was really responsible. Personally I thought they were right and believed them that the person of reference was in this case the active inducer of neurotic behaviour and response. The oblique point made in this part of the discussion was that I was, as explained before, the real provoking agent for their neurotic response. Perhaps I unwittingly repeated the traumatogenic behaviour of the parental figure. Had I been induced to do this? If so, I was not conscious of it.

Another time the conductor had drawn attention to the ways in which patients express their determination to hold on to their neuroses. Words used were 'If you dig your heels in in this way you may very well stay as you are'. This led to a piece of self-analysis on the part of one of the patients who said she had come to realise that she was asking the group to breast feed her. She recognised her own difficulties in breast feeding her daughter in connection with this, and how this affected much of her later relationship with the child. With relation to the group she clearly wanted it to be a better mother to her and she wanted to feel better loved by it, but as it was she was clinging to her neurosis.

Another patient realised that a shift in her interpretation of her own behaviour had taken place; she had previously insisted that the group intervened between her and her home, now she feels it is the boyfriend. She mentions that she is really happier with her boyfriend than at home. She understood this whole affair as a safety valve against certain involvements in the group of which she is afraid.

TRANSFERENCE INTERPRETATIONS: CORRECT, YET DEFENSIVE

The following notes I owe to my co-conductor who took over when I was absent. He was then a learner himself, in personal analysis with someone other than myself. I am sure my colleague, whom I hold in high esteem, will not mind that I use his notes to illustrate a type of interpretation critically, a criticism which the group itself voiced clearly. Obviously the unfavourable comparison which was made between him and me was due to a differential distribution of transference, but nevertheless corresponds to some extent to a real difference in our ways of interpreting. There is also some noticeable group anxiety about my illness and my colleague's way of responding to this is not very reassuring. It can in fact have been only a relatively slight indisposition (such as 'flu or a cold). It is interesting to speculate on a possible implication that the co-conductor might have enhanced the anxiety about my 'illness' quite unconsciously, for reasons of his own, an ambivalence which was very likely stimulated at that time in his own analysis. His own analyst was about my age. The co-conductor knew for instance that he would in any case "inherit" this group from me, and I remember saying to him in our talks after each group session that he gave the impression that he was somewhat impatient for this to happen, which he denied. My main point, however, which was also discussed at the time, is that I believe the transference interpretations here are defensive insofar as they enable the therapist to put it all to the transference of the group, and thus to avoid having to take their criticism seriously.

It seems very difficult for any therapist to avoid such defensiveness and seriously to consider the hints a group gives about his shortcomings.

REPORT

Thursday: Mary B and Dr L were 20 minutes or more late. On my entrance I announced that SHF would not attend and Dr L reported a momentary feeling of relief at SHF's absence. A bit later, he told of an encounter with a nymphomaniac, and his wish to get away and discard her (a social gathering at a pub which might have led to sexual intercourse), and the connection between this confrontation with her sexual challenge, and his confrontation, this time avoided, with SHF as a forbidding father or as a challenging father was evident. Dr L was concerned about SHF's age, and in general there was a feeling that SHF was missed, but yet a denial of what the possible implications were. This became clearer in the next session . . . R saw SHF as avuncular, a kindly and friendly father figure. In an intense exchange with Mrs G both looked into how they handle their angry feelings and some of the fantasies and ideas involved with these. For R, generally overpassive and unable to reach his angry feelings, the ideal is to be able to express them in appropriate circumstances and to the right people, with some freedom. For Mrs G this would lead only to rupture. For her, the angry feelings are too much at hand. She could relate her feelings about anger to her relationship with her mother and father, toward whom anger could not and must not be expressed, because of the inherent danger . . . Essentially, much of the session was spent on an analysis of their feelings about anger and their fears or aspirations about expressing it. O is afraid to do so; R feels it will be the road to liberation. Mrs G fears that it will lead to catastrophe etc. I stress these last points especially in view of material in the next session.

Monday: I reported that SHF was again ill, but could not answer anxious questions about with what or for how long . . . O described at some length how the people to whom he had sold his mother's house (retaining part of the land) had built a garage that infringed on his land by some six feet. His wife was going to hospital for a varicose vein operation, and he would be left to cope. He felt helpless, unable to handle the situation. If she had been there, she would have taken care of the garage matter. He was afraid he couldn't without becoming too destructive, saying: *"How can you be angry with nice people?"* He also brought into account how he felt about being reprimanded by his senior partner, and how this made him feel two years old. There was also a good bit of material about how his feelings oscillated from day to day. One day, he felt two years old, unable to cope; the next morning, he'd awake feeling adult, able to handle things quite well.

I was rather active with O, linking matters with his fears of aggression, with his fears that he could only destroy or submit, and seeking analytic connections in much of his other material, illuminating how essentially his masochism is a defence against his sadistic fantasies. There were several silences from time to time, which I took to be thoughtful ones, and which I twice broke to continue matters, but focussing essentially on O as the group's major spokesman for their fears of expressing anger.

After one of these silences, Mrs G turned on me with a furious verbal attack. I was shutting the group up. I was giving answers, keeping them from finding their own, keeping them from developing. R who in the previous session had said that he thought I was inclined to put things into boxes, joined in somewhat and finally Mary did as well. She would not stay in the group if I were to take over, when SHF retired. Yet she felt that she should not say this, that she owed me a debt of gratitude. As we looked into this, it became quite clear that in transference I was her mother, whom she could not attack face to face because she owed her mother gratitude, and who she felt always judged her. I judged her too, she thought (though I could not find any connection for this in anything I have done in the group). SHF never judges her. The attack on me continued: text book answers, too Freudian, putting closure on things, adding a note of finality. I was too active. SHF was passive, let them grow.

After a bit of this, I connected this with their feelings about SHF's absences which R took up. I believe that at the moment I am Mary's mother, Mrs G's "raping" brother and who knows what to R (he connects me, as does Mrs G with people they encounter in their work and social life, with whom they can't get along). R came to my defence, finally, (as did O, Dr L and M joining in as well), saying that the two techniques could be supplementary. Mary wanted to take back her attack, fearing it might damage me. R recognised that at c e point I looked as if I was hurt by the attack, but that I had recovered. I, admi ting that I had been, that I would have to be very strange not to have felt it, said that it was important that they had been able to attack me, that these feelings had been simmering for a very long time, and that in the exploration and resolution of them might come some very important advances. Certainly, Mary's problem with her mother now has its parallel in her perception of me in the group, ditto Mrs G's feelings about her brother "who always has all the answers".

THE BEGINNING OF A GROUP

This is a somewhat longer example based on notes of a group of my own which lasted more than fifteen years. At these beginning stages it was a group for doctors, psychiatrists, analysts, psychotherapists; also people like sociologists, social workers intended for training. I shall give a condensed account of the first few sessions of this group which will illustrate at the same time how such a group starts and

how various mechanisms operate. This more extensive example will I
think illustrate many of the facets of the conductor's work in the
light of what has been said.

The first session was marked by the unexpected absence of a Dr L who was to
be a participant. Several things were discussed and the group were being taken
into this by being asked to express their feelings, opinions, decisions. At
once a realistic note was introduced in that the group's opinions were taken into
serious consideration and not treated as rhetorical questions or comments. For
example, the question of holidays was discussed and it was agreed that this
group would prefer to close down altogether when there were more than one or
two on holiday. Then I made some remarks about the seating arrangements, and
other arrangements such as not smoking which later led to some rebellion on the
part of one or two. The question of tape-recording was discussed and in effect
rejected by this group, rather surprisingly in that they were all people who were
much concerned with the scientific and theoretical side of the subject. Nevertheless as soon as it came to the personal exposure of themselves a number of
objections were raised. One, Dr M, who came late, very much took the centre of
the stage. This annoyed Dr AR who said so in no uncertain terms. This same Dr
M spoke very much against having a microphone and said he could not resist
hearing his voice all the time and wanted to monopolise the discussion as soon as
there was a microphone. There were various reactions and analytical considerations which arose from this. Another member, Miss G, said that she would not
in the least mind being recorded but that she would mind and she could not
possibly tolerate it if it were replayed. Dr AR made some rather surprising
reflections on his inhibitions especially in relation to a person of authority which
I represented for him. This also referred to all sorts of self-assertiveness on his
part. He described how his heart beat when he had just opposed Dr M for
instance. As a reason for being against recording he gave that he wanted to let
himself go, he hoped to become involved. But as soon as it became "scientific"
or anything like a study group he might just as well attend a scientific meeting.
In this way he voiced a prejudice which is frequently found in these circles,
namely a mutual exclusiveness or at least contrast between emotional and
intellectual attitudes. Even the mere knowledge that something would be
recorded and possibly used scientifically would prevent him from being free.
Now another idea was revealed as being behind this, equally important and
interesting for teaching, namely that he minded very much in his capacity as a
doctor in particular. If anyone could hear and recognise his voice, that would be
disastrous. Something he would mind very much. In former times, before he was
a doctor he did not mind this at all. This naive emotional meaning in fantasy of
being a doctor appeared to me very interesting quite generally. Straight away in
this first session, the fear of the "outside" raised its head. This doctor did not in
the least mind letting himself go in the middle of a group of colleagues or others
in his field, but he was very much afraid of the outside. This differentiation
between inside and outside the group leads to a very interesting problem. In a
deep sense it is related I think to a type of paranoid split. The whole group's
reaction to the idea of "being heard outside" by "outsiders" was very much in
the same direction and this when they knew perfectly well that the material
would only be used with their assent which they really actually had given for

scientific and perfectly legitimate purposes. This session broke up rather abruptly.

The second session: it had become clear that Dr L would not participate. He had obviously changed his mind, giving as reason that he was not well enough. I had in the meantime asked another suitable man to join us and had offered him this vacancy. The group was rather impatient with this new man because he was late. They said: "Will he come now, or not?" With this particular person, latecoming was rather a longstanding symptom, the analysis of which became later on of very decisive importance. When it was analysed in the group it led to a very great and favourable change in his whole life, but the change was a critical one. I can only mention this here because for reasons of discretion I will not be able to go into any detail into this highly interesting material. The total classic anal complexity which was involved came out clearly, and when we come to the point I will indicate this at least in a schematic way. At this point I may only say that one of the inhibitions of this man was that he found it very difficult to complete work and it turned out that in his fantasy as soon as he had completed work he felt he would die. In this second session there was a tense mood at the beginning which I broke by saying "Well, we are not very much at ease". But after that it became lively enough. After some silence Dr M came up with a "group dream": he had in fact had a dream which very obviously referred to the last session and which was to some extent analysed in that sense. Under the circumstances the group participated somewhat less in this than one might have expected and I had correspondingly a little more to do. Even in the manifest dream there was a circle with one empty chair. "It was a circle just like this, but there was one chair which had arms". He at once marched and took this chair and put himself into the centre with the approval of myself and the disapproval of AR. Now Dr AR said he had also had a group dream and that he was most surprised that it was very openly homosexual in relation to me. I gave him an injection in the dream which turned out to be a truth drug. I said this dream was a transference dream in relation to myself and that the emphasis was not so much homosexual but referred to the treatment situation, namely that I would make him speak the truth in the group. The women in the group took up the dream in a lively way; manifestly they were not mentioned. Now the group became very lively and I can only pick out some of the main features. One such feature was a constant wavering between taking things intellectually and quite genuinely plunging into things in a personal way. The group seemed to understand it as their function to make remarks which referred to their mutual interrelationship. At the same time there was considerable uncertainty and guessing about my own role, and a lot of prejudice about that. I tried to break through this by saying "Who told you that?" or "Who says this?" I took in fact a very free part. I did not at all confirm various anticipations of my sort of sacrosanct position. When I say a "free part" I do not mean that I volunteered material in a personal way but I gave evidence of what I thought as a group member, what I felt, and I was participating in the deliberations. I partly did this because the group was not as ready and free to do it themselves as they might have been. I also noted that two or three times I said in a sort of apologetic way "I'm sorry I say so much" something which I had not entirely intended to say in just that way. One of the things which now occupied us was rebelling about not smoking — the question about natural and artificial situations. The discussion tended to become rather technical. A woman doctor, Anita, raised a point about her individual analyst. Two or three of the participants were having individual analysis with other analysts, though this was the tail end of it. At that time I still accepted this situation. She (Anita) had seemed to have settled this question but now raised it rather suddenly in a way which seemed almost to question her whole participation, reflecting also resistances on the part of her own analyst. She eventually came to an agreement with the analyst about this.

Apart from those still in analysis, others had had an analysis. Questions frequently arose such as "What has your analysis shown about that?" So I had to intervene and say "Let us find all this out here". This doctor, Anita, who almost provoked me to rebuke her, in confronting her with the tendency to turn the discussion on to a technical level, suddenly said rather apologetically: "Does it take too much time to talk about a personal matter which is very much in my mind?" I naturally said that this was precisely what we were here for. She now told a story which was only a day or two old — namely that a married man with whom she had had relations for 9 months, had suddenly turned this off and declared it was wrong. (Such sudden changes in reactions on the part of the other members of a patient's intimate network, his plexus, happen not infrequently and are part and parcel of the ongoing therapy.) All this came about in connection with a patient. Her friend was a practitioner and this patient was his as well as hers at the same time, so that they treated her in common. This patient had a sort of mirror story to theirs. The GP when he saw her guilty reaction took that to heart and said to Anita "It is not right — we must give it up" (that is to say, their relationship.) Anita was very preoccupied with this. She felt like killing him but she felt she couldn't get at him and she was also at the same time afraid that she might break him. She seemed full of conflict about this. In all this she did not show too much insight. For instance, no insight at all into the possibility that this whole matter might have occurred to her just now through some unconscious influence on her own part. I was myself convinced that this was so and many in the group were too.

This enabled Miss G to bring forth something intimate concerning herself. She said: "I have a similar story — somebody ran away from me but I am quite convinced that I did it myself". This highly cathexed matter arose in Anita as follows. She also had opposed the verdict on smoking but it *wasn't smoking which mattered* but that she could not bear that somebody was in charge of her, *that he was able to take something away from her*, to just stop it, in other words, a deep-going meaning of oral frustration in her whole character entering into the Transference (T) situation. At this stage the whole group expressed how exceptionally well they felt about each other. This was unusual for them, particularly Dr Anita and also I think Miss J and Miss G. They gave as the reasons for this that they were all familiar with psychoanalysis and therefore knew what they were talking about. To my mind this was a rationalisation, to cover some deeper meaning but I did not want to mention this.

When I indicated to Dr Anita that her impulsive basic reactions, the character basis, was really the problem and not really this particular experience, she felt that she really ought to be able to talk it over and talk it out with the man himself. Thus I had to mention that all individual as well as group-analytic treatment was based particularly on the fact that this sort of talking out can best be done in such a situation as this one, rather than with the person himself concerned. This remark was more in place in a group of this composition than it might otherwise have been. It sheds light on one of the basic assumptions of all group analysis – on the fact that people are intimate strangers, and are in a certain sense nearer to the transference person than to the actual person in life. Vice versa they should not, as so frequently happens, transpose the habit of talking things out into ordinary life situations which are quite different. I am not quite clear how much of this went home but in my own mind I linked it up with an experience in another group between SJ and Mrs A who took each other as proxies for their respective marital partners and in this way went much deeper into things than they could with their actual marital partners. They commented on this repeatedly quite spontaneously.

Now a last word on a very interesting point. When I indicated that the really irritating frustrating point for Anita was that somebody else had power onesidedly to terminate a desire of hers, such as I had done over the smoking, she quite agreed with me. She then immediately jumped back, saying "Yes, I was rather suddenly weaned, I was born in South Africa, and was rather suddenly weaned and lost the breast early". This remark although true and relevant was nevertheless, I considered, conditioned by her knowledge of a certain type of psychoanalytical interpretation. Now Dr AR raised a few theoretical questions concerning this spontaneous jump into early oral pathology or experience, namely whether this was regression and above all "What can one do? What can one do if things go back so far?" It was clear that this theoretical point was emotionally highly cathexed and this was confirmed much later in the course of this treatment. I pointed out that one could do something however early were the original impressions which caused certain behaviour. If they were still at the root of present difficulties or conflicts now one must also be able to get hold of them here and now. (He then branched off in rather theoretical terms about regression, fixation, etc. which I felt I had to take up a little in the circumstances.) This provoked some protest from Miss G who said she could not follow, and also from SA who protested against making this into a theoretical discussion. AR then confirmed that all sorts of things depended on the answer to his question. For instance, should he give up his own analysis? In fact I am sure that this was highly cathexed emotional material for him in his analysis. There he was putting his problem into theoretical terms about which as a matter of fact he was not very clear. Actually he did later decide to give up his psychoanalysis in favour of the group, and he also decided to get married. The marriage so far as I know was quite a happy one, but nevertheless we are right to be careful about such decisions taken while things are still stirred up by an on-going analytical approach or even some time after this. In this particular case, the problem arose more from his own individual psychoanalysis than from the group situation, but in later years I would not have accepted this situation at all in which somebody attends one of my groups while he is still in individual analysis with another therapist.

This type of group which comprised people in the profession who had had psychoanalytical experience in their own person shows a particular ambivalence between knowing and not knowing theoretically at the same time. As Dr M quite rightly remarked "There you are, you see, these [technical] terms are non-sensical – only used defensively and it would be far better to know nothing at all – it only prevents one". Last time, he had also shown a certain ambivalence in connection with the intellectual-versus-emotional conflict. He asked whether all were familiar with this jargon so that one could use it as a short cut. This theme had been mentioned by Drs AR and N right at the beginning of this session, and came up now almost like a piece of music. These two doctors impersonated this conflict at the same time, with ever-changing roles and sides.

In the next session, the third, one of the members began to take on a kind of "conductor's assistant" role. The group was altogether extremely lively, Dr M being rather aggressive but in a good humoured way. Members spontaneously contributed in a lively manner and presented a beautiful analytical picture. One talked about anxiety and fear of what happens to one and "this can happen to anyone". The same member mentioned that before the session his car broke down and he had to 'phone that he would have to be late. Another member of the group reported that he couldn't "do a thing except at the last moment". She talked quite unaware in terms like "I sit down and nothing will come" and "I have not a thought in my mind, I just feel empty — I cannot produce anything". She gave almost a classic example of an anal interpretation. This provoked a lot of resistances from others who said "This could have many interpretations". Somebody talked about his annoyance about "the loss of money" when he missed a session. Group cohesion — in spite of the absence on holiday of the conductor — was the main content of another group dream. She said that it was extraordinary how she knew in the dream ("How clearly one knows such things in a dream!") — namely about this bond that existed although she said "It is very difficult to express or explain". Some in the group found this difficult to understand — one of them said "Is it really so clear in a dream? Does one know it really so clearly?"

I should like at this point to reproduce my own observation and notes to this at the time: "Now this sort of very concrete yet intangible quality plays a great role in my own way of imagining things, and therefore it is a very easy thing for me to understand what she meant. I must find a word for that sometime. I would have been inclined to call it 'spiritual' if this term had not other connotations."

Concerning this anal meaning of production, which was shared by the whole group, it is perhaps good to emphasise three elements provisionally: those of producing something, something original, something which comes out of oneself; producing it on request at a certain time and place, and with a view of publication. It is as if someone was demanding or expecting it or waiting for it. This is very important. The one who fears, as already mentioned, that he would die when his work was complete, expressed clearly the narcissistic aspect which was also linked with paranoid mechanisms and that the publicly waiting person becomes the person of reference, a kind of bête noire. He then mentioned a current example of this, and not surprisingly, the man to whom he referred was related to one of the women group members. In such a group things are at the same time enacted, they are expressed in action inside or outside the group, preferably the two being linked with each other. Further elements of this total complex are mentioned by one or two others who are always losing things. One said "I can't find it". The other always loses her watch — now for the third time, and said "One always blames someone else, one feels one is being persecuted — one dreams sometimes 'who has taken this away? Who is it now?' " We know these observations very well from experience in life as well as in psychotherapy.

As regards the theme of dying, this was taken up by Dr ON. He spoke of a legendary theme, as for instance the idea of the swan song, the theme of somebody dying when he has done his real work — his real masterpiece. We also spoke of ideas of somebody doing a wonderful work, and is then killed. I myself remembered being told as a child by my aunt that the man who completed the clock in the Münster in Strasbourg was blinded after having done this work. I may have actually mentioned this. Miss G said "Yes the most wonderful member or person is always sacrificed". In this connection another legend was mentioned, that pain must be suffered for the acquisition of knowledge. The knowledge must be stolen from the gods, therefore the pain is in the nature of a punishment. "Do you really believe this to be true?" asked Dr M and the member who had brought this forth was rather taken aback. However he defended himself against opinions that his convictions should be confused with the collective unconscious of Jung. Whereupon Dr M whose own analyst was Jungian said: "Because you think it is all Jungian nonsense."

It is hoped that even this very sketchy reproduction of my notes which were in lieu of recording will give an idea of what is meant by resonance, by the key note, usually quite unconscious, often on different levels at the same time, and which often permeates the productions of a group and gives the basis for the conductor as to when to interpret what is really going on.

An attempt to represent the foregoing material graphically is shown in Chart 3 (p. 152).

In the fourth session questions of authority or defiance of authority were raised. Questions of impatience in a group, of aggression, of "having gloves off" and so forth. Correspondingly, a great deal of dissatisfaction with me was expressed in the sense that group treatment did not help. This appeared to me in the sharpest possible contrast with my own observations, to my considered view of this group. There was of course considerable ambivalence about this; some definitely voicing that they had benefitted greatly already, that it was very helpful to them. They spoke of the great relief it is to talk over certain things which are so much tied up in one, so that there was at the same time as much feeling of satisfaction.

The following sessions were in no way less interesting, quite on the contrary. I will restrict myself to giving a short outline in order to let the reader know how things continued. In the fifth session, the group expressed or showed strong hostility towards me and at the same time took up the question of death, of my death in particular, of the suicide of a patient, and one member reported that she had nearly not come because her own father had died the previous Friday. The group had ignored me as far as possible, and treated me as non-existent, and everybody became more-or-less an assistant conductor. In the sixth session I addressed the group as a whole and pointed this out which was followed by a number of individual responses, the group becoming rather lively and productive. My rather massive intervention directed to the group as a whole was in this case unquestionably correct in the situation. In the seventh session a great deal of hostility was actually voiced in relation to myself. I appeared as somebody who rebuked members. There were some quite aggressive outbursts against me and the particular rebellion against me as a father figure was taken up by one of the members in whom it was the most outspoken feature. This same man reported in the eighth session that he actually felt much better, he had seen his analyst again in the country during the week and had told him so and at the same time a lot of dependence on me was expressed. In the following (ninth) session, one of the features was that open paranoid experiences and interpre-

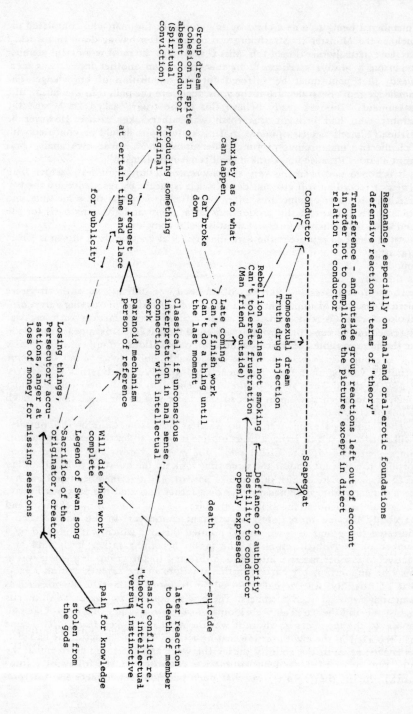

tations of peoples' behaviour broke through in one of the members but this was a break through in a favourable sense. These paranoid features again had interesting resonances in others. A number of psychotic relationships and affects were brought to discussion. In the tenth session, apart from these psychotic relations — it was remarkable how many had got what one of them called "suicidal people as skeletons in the cupboard". I would like to mention that one member said he felt a feeling of elation in the group — just as he had felt as a child in church. This feeling of hilarity and exhilaration was difficult to disguise, and then he made a particular remark that he felt this "behind his eyes". This struck me because this is the very point mentioned, after very long study by Trigant Burrow, this peculiar feeling behind the eyes. I did not however mention this.

In order to round up my report on this group or rather on its beginning I would like to mention two particular events:

1) One of the women members, Miss G turned out to be suffering from cancer. It was the group which had helped her for the first time to realise that she must see a doctor in connection with this. This led to her being operated upon. Later on, she had a relapse of lung cancer and unfortunately died. This was the only experience I have made of this kind and I think I have recorded elsewhere how significant the reactions of the individual members to this experience were. Each reaction was in line with each individual's psychopathology. This is what one would expect. But the material was most fascinating in this respect. A factual event, which had made a great impact on the group was here the common basis of this resonance.

2) The other observation I want to report is that I became fully aware for the first time in this group of the mechanism of scapegoating. This scapegoat was in fact the victim of aggression, of destructive energies which were really directed towards me, the conductor. Before this time I had only noticed that I had always an instinctive wish, which I also sometimes followed, to come to the rescue of the scapegoat. I proceeded to analyse the group in connection with their attacks, but I was not then fully aware that I did so basically as a countertransference reaction. In this particular group I became aware of this clearly and acted upon this insight.

MAXIMS

Now here are, by way of maxims, a few disjointed remarks on the conductor's functions, or principles, to serve as a brief memo of what he sets out to do, how he might go about it, or how he should not go about it.

1) Prepare yourself well. Your own knowledge is never finally achieved. You are continuously working at yourself in your activity and function. Your conducting is a continuous learning, but this should not be at the expense of the group.

2) You should not have to communicate to the group in order to satisfy your own needs, such as relieving your own anxieties.

3) Try and understand the principles of the group-analytic situation. You have to create this and actively maintain it in your function as an adminstrator and as a responsible director and guide

4) Always follow the group. Listen before you intervene. When you think you understand listen again and see whether it is confirmed.

5) It is *not* your usual function to communicate your insight to the group, to interpret. See whether they don't themselves find the solution, and if not, why not. You may sometimes gently help, if that is necessary. Do *not* use analysing and interpreting — especially historical interpreting — as a defence.

6) Try to find out why and how the group goes about it *not* to understand. (By the way, also how each patient goes about it not to change.) In the analysis of these blocs or resistances you can be more active and help to unearth the unconscious reasons for them. If they are shared, point them out to all, to the group as a whole, by confrontation, analysis of behaviour as well as by interpretation.

7) All interpretations in the broadest sense, indeed all observations are based in the first place on the group as a whole, in the group context. It is here where the figure/ground orientation and the correct location of disturbances becomes important. This is not the same as saying that interpretations must necessarily be addressed to the group as a whole.

8) For optimal treatment do not go on too long. Take sufficient time and care to introduce the patient and to work through the ending of treatment with the patient. At all times analyse any request or apparent need for individual appointments within the group session itself if at all possible.

9) Focus on the patient's need to be ill, to defend his illness and on his self-destruction. Do not be manoeuvred into being responsible for curing him. You must also show him that you are *not* his father, mother etc.

10) What to do with reactions to the patients' challenges and provocations? A group of patients will put you to a strong test. It will spot your weak points as if it were a collective genius in psychology. You must deal with these hurts and pains by your own mental hygiene. It is not necessarily the best answer from time to time to undergo an analysis again. It may be better to discuss such strains with understanding colleagues mutually, maybe in scientific and technical terms, and have a kind of free group discussion about them.

If you are a reasonably healthy and emotionally balanced person, your life itself and your interests should help you to put these traumas to your self-esteem into proper perspective.

11) If you conduct the group according to the principles laid down in this book and in the spirit of these maxims you should become a stronger and better therapist as well as person. A genuine theoretical and philosophical interest in the whole subject helps, I think, greatly in achieving the right equilibrium between the human involvement and the desirable detachment. Such interest allows one to see the general, universal, importance of what is going on, rather than merely the detail which demands one's immediate attention.

CHAPTER 7

The Conductor As A Person And His Training

We will consider here the personal qualities, desirable and undesirable, of a future group analyst.

His personality is indeed important, as the whole style in which he conducts his groups depends upon this. I would give a very high priority to the trainee's ethical integrity. The group analyst has a very high degree of responsibility to those who entrust themselves to his care. This transcends what one would call the medical responsibility, as we shall presently see.

His interest in his subject must be genuine. He must not be overweighted with motives such as "helping other people" because this is too often based on deep-seated individual motivations and even unresolved conflicts. This is not desirable. His interest should be of a more detached, sublimated kind, similar to that of a scientist or artist. A psychological bent of mind and gift is essential, whether inborn or acquired early is insignificant; probably it is both as usual.

To me the role of a conductor in a group-analytic group has always appeared to be similar to that of a poet or writer in the community. He should be receptive to the current problems of his time and creative in expressing them in such a way as to bring them nearer to the consciousness of those concerned. I need hardly mention that good intelligence is necessary as is the capacity for understanding and for making oneself understood in simple terms. Commonsense, that uncommon commodity, is important. All these characteristics may develop and mature fully only in training and the formation which comes through actual work with patients.

One particular capacity can hardly be overrated: it is that of being able to listen receptively, to keep in reserve one's own expectations or biases. At the same time there must be a capacity to have a very active and open mind to the manifold ramifications of what is being observed. This combination is not frequent.

Honesty towards oneself and others is fundamental. There must be a love of truth, even if it is disagreeable and contrary to personal advantage. Nothing has impressed me more than the degree to which people bend their minds, their emotions, their convictions, their opinions, even the very structure of their minds, according to their personal advantages or disadvantages, and changes of all sorts in their fortunes. This is often quite manifest and clear, but people in general are very strongly defended against admitting this to themselves and correcting such a faulty bias.

The future therapist should himself be mentally and emotionally balanced and able to lead a full life with sufficient breadth of interests in order to have experience with the world and with people. By this I do not mean that he should be a gregarious socialite, but a man open to new experiences and who is able to learn from them and to give himself a chance to experience his own responses to very different situations. He should be reasonably free from neurotic or psychotic disturbances or character malformations and from gross sexual deviations. He will be greatly helped in all this by insight into the power of his own unconscious motivations and his personal experience with the significance of transference phenomena, an essential part of his training.

The atmosphere created in therapeutic groups must allow for the experience of helplessness, hopelessness and despair in safety. In such a situation the group turns to a leader as a god to give it strength. True education ("Bildung") will prevent the therapist from the temptation to succumb to his power drive or omnipotent fantasies, or to have undue therapeutic ambition. In facing groups there are certain typical anxieties, especially in the beginner, which have to do with the unconscious assumption in the conductor that he has to be perfect, or even omniscient or omnipotent. These are his own unconscious presumptions as well and no wonder he feels afraid. The truly genuine person will not fear being seen as he is. He will have no undue expectations of having to be perfect and he will share the humility and modesty which as human people we have every reason to have.

Whatever his own tastes and political convictions as a citizen, he must be liberal enough in a deep sense to treat all human people in his group as equal. This does not mean that they are not very different on a realistic level. Some are attractive and charming, understanding; others difficult and annoying; some are influential and rich and others miserable creatures and even ugly. He need not blind himself to this, but in a profound sense we are equal human people. One might almost say "equal" in a spiritual sense. This brings me to the question of religion.

Religion, if it is worth anything, must be sincere and deeply believed. It is difficult to envisage that such a religious person could help wishing to form other people in the same spirit. This, however, as we have emphasised, is undesirable. This objection does not hold good for those priests or ministers who wish to use group-analytic insight or even training in the work with their own religious confrères. There we must assume that all are agreed on the wish to share in the same religious spirit. It must also be said that there are equally deep-going attachments outside religion in the fanatic adherence to certain convictions, including the quasi-religious adherence to any particular psychological school. There is another objection to religion in the sense of denomination or of any system of religion existing in the world, namely that as true scientists, it is hard for us to treat any such religious system differently from any other mythology or superstitious belief. It is equally true that in view of the many trials and tribulations of life, it is far more difficult to live without any such system than it is to live with it. However, while as scientists we cannot well be true adherents to a particular religious system, the artistic side in us, the creative side, is a full equivalent for us. This is all the more the case as our very work enables us to make full use of this side. In the end it comes down to what Goethe said so simply: "Who possesses science and art is religious, he who does not possess both of these should have religion."

Having outlined what the conductor as a person should be, we cannot avoid saying something about what he should *not* be. Obviously, the first answer to this is that he should not be the opposite of what we have just discussed as being desirable, but more particularly we should rule out people who are pervert to a marked degree — for instance, sadists, homosexuals, those who are paranoid, those who lead a neurotic life, are members of a highly neurotic plexus and not able to free themselves from this. We do not want people who are out for their own advantage, material or otherwise, those who are vain and oversensitive, fanatic, and those who think they have a mission to fulfil.

THE TRAINING OF GROUP ANALYSTS

Selection of Candidates

On the basis of the general human foundation which we have just reviewed, we come now to the selection of candidates for training. We may assume that most really unsuitable people would rule themselves out, that is to say, they would not come our way. If they did they would be easily recognised. Otherwise candidate selection in many ways is not dissimilar to that of patients. We have spoken of the importance of general education and of course some kind of evidence, like an academic degree might have to be used as a check. The group analyst like the psychoanalyst has much to know in such disciplines as sociology, anthropology, biology, philosophy, history, politics, economic life, literature, art. However, apart from his special priorities, a basic familiarity with the most important aspects in these respects might suffice. We have of course to consider the special significance of a medical degree as such, a psychiatric training more particularly, and training in psychoanalysis.

Medical Degree

Merits It is of course important if the future candidate is familiar with medical illnesses from a somatic and a psychosomatic point of view. The basic knowledge of anatomy, but particularly of physiology is important and even more so the biological orientation which the medical student brings with him. Obviously much of the medical education is not needed — for instance knowledge of surgery, knowledge of fractures and dislocations, of infectious diseases, of gynaecology or midwifery. An exception, albeit a very important one, is the psychiatric training and quite particularly an intimate personal acquaintance with psychotic patients, with the wide range of conditions which the psychiatrist meets, which is not otherwise obtainable. I am obviously talking of a living form of psychiatry, dynamic psychiatry as it has been called. Where medical education as such is absent, and psychiatric experience in particular, definite limitations are set for the future psychotherapist's range.

Drawbacks The medical discipline is per se almost antipsychological in its orientation, except in relatively few teachers who have a particular gift and interest in this respect. The medical model itself built on concepts of normality, illness and cure is not well suited to the tasks of the future psychotherapist, psychoanalyst or group analyst. Fortunately it is possible to develop an organismic model of thinking which does not have these drawbacks, and which inside medicine ipso facto includes the human psychological factors.

On the whole there is no question that medical education, including psychiatric education in particular, is an asset and that its advantages outweigh its disadvantages if any. Seeing that in the nature of the problems we have to deal with, persons not medically qualified are inevitably drawn into this work in increasing numbers, it can only be hoped that facilities can be provided for them to learn at least the most important lessons with which the medical student is familiar.

Psychoanalytic Training

Pros and Cons There is no question that psychoanalytical training, including experience in one's own person, is very desirable. In a sense, it is indispensable but we will have to look into the situation more closely. If our candidate has already undergone such training, in other words if he is an experienced psychoanalyst already, so much the better. There is no problem then though it is still an exception for a trained psychoanalyst to become seriously devoted to group analysis. If rightly understood it clashes in no way with his own psychoanalytic activities. A point of great importance is the risk that the trained psychoanalyst is hampered by the built-in limitations of his own system. This can be overcome and completely solved but many people are not able to do so. Even in the fully trained psychoanalyst, personal group-analytic experience and training remains essential.

What we have to know from psychoanalysis above all is the early development of both sex and ego: the universal power of self-destructive instincts: the structural model of personality: the total psychology as embedded in Freud's researches on the dream: the approach to the dynamic unconscious in view of the classical form of resistances and defences, broadly speaking, of repression. Independent of this, a dynamic acquaintance with the unconscious, though not repressed functions of the ego and the super-ego, and last but not least familiarity with transference both from the point of view of the patient and the psychoanalyst, countertransference, and as a result of all this, the acquisition of what I have termed the "analytic attitude".

If our candidate has not had this experience, he might acquire sufficient of it in his own group analysis, provided this is intensive and extensive enough. Even then he might complete his training in analytic respects by an individual analytic experience of his own. In my opinion, which I have often expressed, the sequence would better be as indicated here: to undergo group analysis first, and then work this experience through in the two person situation. It would be desirable that this analysis should not be as prolonged as is often the case in professional psychoanalysts, but should be more in the nature of one to two years in length. One thing is certain: one cannot learn this from books alone. It should however be stressed that we cannot learn it either from experience alone. Intensive study and work are necessary, reading and thinking in addition to personal experience.

As I have indicated, the especial merits of personal psychoanalytic training are obvious but there are certain potential drawbacks also in the fully trained psychoanalyst. It should be remarked that the fully trained psychoanalyst, whoever he might be, (even if we confined ourselves to the Freudian school entirely) as a rule is inevitably very much influenced by the special ideas and convictions of his training analyst, so that any two psychoanalysts may differ considerably from each other.

Taking a broader view, what is really necessary is that the therapist has arrived at a balanced capacity to deal with difficult patients in an analytic spirit, in a psychotherapeutic spirit as modelled by the psychoanalytic school in particular. These qualifications are in any case equally essential for his activities in the individual as well as in the group situation, indeed experiences in a group situation make a very significant contribution to training which nobody who is only familiar with the two person situation can acquire to the same extent. One could, therefore, very well turn the matter round and say that the future psychoanalyst should have a fundamental training in group analysis, if possible prior to his psychoanalytical training.

A Training Scheme For Future Group Analysts Which Can Be Modified To Include Future Group Psychotherapists.

What I have said hitherto about the general human preconditions in the selection of personalities for this profession and the selection of candidates is of course a somewhat idealised programme which we cannot expect in every case to realise fully. I will continue to talk about training here in the same spirit, namely that of an optimal model under the best conditions. We will then have to consider what by contrast are the minimal conditions which we expect and on which we would have to insist. It seems obvious therefore that most people will be somewhere on a range between these two extremes. The following training scheme should therefore be understood in this light.

In any training scheme it is necessary to be very careful in the selection of personalities and the finer selection as to their inner preparation as has been indicated in the above. It is important to take sufficient time and trouble in this selection. In addition to the personal psychopathology of the candidate, his plexus and other networks and the problems with which they present him and the way he does or does not solve them must also be considered. In practical terms it might be desirable, as in the case of a patient, to examine not only the candidate himself but the relevant people of his family and others in his intimate network and plexus.

The first and foremost need is to insist on his participating as a full member in a therapeutic group. Obviously if he wants to be a group analyst this group should be conducted by a fully competent group analyst. This training should be thorough and it is likely to take three years. There are pros and cons to having such candidates in special groups together, or the opposite: as I have indicated, I have had experience with both these methods and both have their problems and both are not ideal. If there is sufficient choice of training group analysts, it is perhaps slightly preferable to have the future candidate mixed up with an ordinary patients' group, which of course should be one that is suitable for him. The first year, roughly, of this group experience should be considered as further diagnostic information and assessment. This should not be made too explicit as otherwise the training analyst is brought too much into the situation of a tester or judge, which is not desirable. The best is perhaps to be non-commital and to say to the future candidate that he should first of all now join such a group. His readiness for undergoing this is in itself an important test of the seriousness of his intentions. On the whole the problems which are still unresolved are not different from those which are unresolved in psychoanalytical training.

Let us assume that after about a year the candidate is recommended by his therapist for further training, or for training at all. In that case he should be seen or seen again by one or two other consultants, possibly the one who saw him first of all and who can form an independent judgement. If he is then accepted, he may be given to understand that he can continue with the prospect of becoming a group analyst, although there cannot at any stage be a definite commitment on the part of anyone concerned. At about this time, allowing for sufficient flexibility in the situation for the different candidates, he may start to sit in with another therapist, so as to observe an on-going group of which he is not a patient member but a participant observer. If and when the teaching analyst who conducts this particular group feels the time is ripe, the candidate may then be entrusted with running a group by himself under supervision. He can start reading the relevant literature after the first year, but more systematic theoretical teaching should only begin after this time, say, after two years. In this way, we can also take into account the experiences and problems arising from the candidate's own experience as an assistant co-conductor and as a conductor under supervision. The theoretical instruction should then still continue, quite particularly when the candidate begins to conduct groups by himself under personal supervision and later without this.

Here is perhaps the place to mention the auxiliary methods which are certainly very valuable, when they are obtainable, and which in my opinion have greater importance for training than they have for treatment. Here belongs the one-way screen with its obvious possibilities, tape-recording, and particularly videotape. The use which can be made of these as auxiliary means of learning, and also of research, need not occupy us further here.

Having outlined a scheme under optimal conditions and for the optimal training of a group analyst, let us consider how much we have to insist upon as a minimum training. Concessions must be made concerning practical difficulties not evoked by the candidate, and we must look upon the whole matter in the light of omissions which can be of a complementary nature. That is to say, if we have great positive signs, such as special gifts or a specially suitable personality on the one side, we may be able to give more on the other. For instance, some people may not have had a psychoanalytical training – in that case their own group analysis becomes of greater importance; vice versa, under exceptional circumstances, one might waive the demand for lengthy personal group analysis in a candidate who is well trained and experienced in psychoanalysis and who shows particular interest and inclination to extend his range to groups and the ability to learn what he can when he can. We are still at a stage of development in this field when we have quite often to compromise and deviate from the optimal course; what is worse is that those available as teachers have often not themselves had the optimal training. If on the other hand the experience is full, we might in the circumstances let the future group analyst off theoretical training, especially when he shows every sign that he does his homework in that respect himself.

I have indicated that medical and psychiatric training may have to be missed, but that this should set certain limitations on the range of patients who can be treated. In a similar way, if certain shortcomings in both psychoanalytic and group-analytic respects cannot be avoided, we may still be able to have a good person to practise a less exacting type of group psychotherapy, if he modifies his treatment accordingly and avoids getting involved in water deeper than is good for him or for his patients. Such group psychotherapists should not be looked upon as "second-rate citizens" as it were. Group psychotherapy of a less specifically analytical kind is a method of considerable value and greatly needed, indeed in quite a number of situations, it is actually more desirable than a fully fledged group analysis. Furthermore, the group psychotherapist I have in mind here may, at a later stage, qualify fully as a group analyst.

The main overall capacity which should have been cultivated and preserved is the capacity to learn, that is to change one's attitude according to one's experiences and insights, to remain flexible over one's convictions and to overcome the defences and resistances against learning in the more profound meaning of this term. Putting it differently, if a man has preserved this capacity and develops it through his training, and is capable of developing it further with his own work, he will belong to those who become better as they go along. If he has not that capacity he will inevitably get stuck, regress, deteriorate as a therapist and probably get into personal trouble.

Having set our sights rather high, but in no way exaggerately so, for this profession, let me end this paragraph with a personal remark, which I am sure applies to others as well. I think that ours is a very beautiful and creative work. Personally I would not change with anyone or change it for any other. This work is in living material not like that of the sculptor or artist or actor. A director in the theatre or a film producer has to work as it were with puppets or trained actors instead of living persons. Even "psychodrama" is based on enacting, on role-playing, and not on life itself as is our work. I found that my very considerable interest for the theatre has somewhat diminished as in many ways a play, unless of the first rank, fails in comparison with the drama of reality in front of me. We need not, like Prometheus, form men in our image but in theirs, to help them to become what they are, to use Nietzsche's dictum. Their personalities emerge all of their own. Method must not be a strait jacket, although its roots and its principles should be understood and respected, each has his own style. One patient who at one time could not face the group without me said, after I had analysed this with her later on, "It is not what you do but what you are which seems essential". It of course included what she had made out of me but it also meant me, and I was pleased. But this is not reserved for me personally. It applies to anyone as soon as he has the courage to be what he is as a conductor too.

CHAPTER 8

On Teaching Psychotherapy

A. TEACHING AND PSYCHOTHERAPY

These are related processes; better perhaps to say they are over-lapping and have their fundamental mechanisms in common. Simple facts or skills may be taught by a teacher to a pupil in more-or-less didactic form and by example. Even in this case, as we know, the personal relationship which forms between pupil and teacher is of paramount importance. As soon as we are concerned with teaching or learning quite new perspectives, the situation becomes different because to learn quite new facts or aspects in regard to any subject we have to change our attitude beyond the facts under consideration themselves. We are then, as Mrs. Abercrombie has so convincingly demonstrated, up against old notions and attitudes. The teaching/learning process is one and the same. The teacher must in turn be a good learner in understanding the pupils' difficulties. Vice versa we understand from this point of view that undergoing psychotherapy of a more intensive kind, especially of course of an analytic type, can be also described as a learning process, even more as an *unlearning* process. This in more conventional analytic language would correspond to the analytic resolution of defences and resistances, and in structural language it would be the modification by analysis of unconscious ego and super-ego functions. Both psychotherapy and teaching are therefore ultimately concerned with the question of change of attitude in the whole person.

If we teach psychotherapy itself this is certainly a matter of intensive personal involvement and the didactic method or learning from books is by itself almost useless. Psychotherapy can best be taught in the ongoing process of a therapeutic situation.

B. RESISTANCES

It may be useful if we look specifically on the resistances to change, resistances to learning — the causes of which must be undone in a process of unlearning.

a) Resistances against being told By this I mean being told anything by anyone. This resistance is most marked between two men which has to do with it being felt by the learner as a dependency relationship, as a kind of submission. The male to male submission is a particularly sensitive area because of the unconscious sexual libidinal connotation. In other words it is a narcissistic hurt for many or even most to be taught at all by another person. One should therefore never try to teach unless specifically asked, and avoid becoming too interested in the trainee's learning.

b) Against learning We have already explained this. The old is in the way of the new. It is mainly the defence against unlearning. This one can help by interpretation, confrontation and in the psycho-therapeutic situation by analysis.

c) Against the change of attitude required Only what has been learned as the result of a change in attitude lasts. The best prescription for the teacher against this type of difficulty is that he practises what he teaches in his supervisory function, that he himself shows a readiness to change and to look upon new and unexpected facets.

d) Resistances which refer more specifically to the therapeutic relationship These of course comprise all that part (the most important one) of analysis which is concerned with the defences, the unconscious influence of the ego's structure, the super-ego's inhibiting functions. This refers to any new insights but even more so if we are not concerned with a neutral or apparently neutral subject matter but with the patient himself. To this must be added the transference reaction of the patient which is ultimately the most powerful resistance of all, a final attempt to retain the basic neurosis intact. It is important in dealing with all these resistances to be always as concrete and to the point as possible; in close touch with the front-line as it were of the defence, with the front-line of the difficulty, so as to get under one's patients' skins.

We must focus on the situation of the trainee in which these processes are highlighted. The special usefulness of the group situation for both teaching and therapy is our central theme in this book. This the more so if one's subject matter is, or at any rate includes, teaching trainees in group psychotherapy in particular. I will therefore in the following give an outline of a method I have used and found very useful, and highlight the principles of it.

Our trainees have their own therapeutic problems, not only in the sense that they need therapy or analysis from a therapeutic point of view but quite particularly also as future therapists. According to the model of psychoanalysis which to some extent we maintain in group analysis a special situation is reserved for the therapeutic analysis itself. This is supplemented later on by various supervisory experiences. Just as a patient, after an analysis, needs some time — half a year or a year or so, before he can really be said to have "finished with his analysis" — so the future analyst (individual or group) also needs a number of years at the very least of being a self-responsible analyst until his training is completed. This dual approach, moving in stages, in overlapping stages, from being a patient to being a trainee, to being a therapist under supervision and eventually to being a therapist without supervision, seems to be the best we can so far devise, but it does not solve the problem of training psychotherapists who do not wish to undergo the total specialist training of the psychoanalyst or group analyst respectively.

Under these conditions, with which I was concerned at the Maudsley Hospital for fifteen years, the question arises whether we can train doctors who wish to be effective psychotherapists in one integrated situation. Can this be done? I believe so, on the basis of the type of supervisory group which I conducted, and according to all participants, with notable success. This group was discussed extensively in Chapter XX of my book *Therapeutic Group Analysis*; here I will confine myself to the most salient points. This teaching group was an alternative to Balint's type of group with general practitioners which co-incided in time. I have not seen any of Balint's groups myself, but think they were quite differently conducted from mine. Occasionally, we had members who had had experiences in both types of group and who seemed to get more out of this free discussion type of group-analytic experience. Balint's groups were directed to teach general practitioners whereas my students were post-graduate trainees who already had considerable psychiatric experience, or who had psychoanalytic experience, or who intended to become psychoanalysts themselves. My own impression is that with Balint the use of the group situation was more or less incidental, whereas with the group I am talking about here it was the other way round. It was a teaching situation very consciously and precisely derived from the particular characteristics of that group situation.

It is just that point which I wish to illustrate here as an example of a fundamental group-analytic principle. The boundaries of the group were clearly established and dynamically maintained. In simply describing this teaching group in all its conditions, it is hoped that this is understood also as an illustration, as a pattern of what we should do with any group situation in which we work.

As already mentioned, the participants were registrars, bent on learning something about psychotherapy. They themselves conducted groups as well as individual psychotherapy at the same time and the purpose of this supervisory seminar was for them to derive the maximum benefit and to learn as much as possible from their on-going experience as therapists. They were usually between five and seven in number, apart from occasional visitors. They met regularly with me once a week, sitting around in an informal circle in the group room of the hospital, and we spent a whole session, that is to say 2½ to 3 hours, for this purpose. They brought with them the attendance sheets of their respective patients' groups; and anything from two to four of such groups were reported on each time. The atmosphere was informal and mutual discussion was encouraged. This group of registrars knew each other well. They were colleagues, friends, in some respects rivals outside this situation. For this reason, I avoided going into any private personal matters. It was quite clear therefore that it differed from a psychotherapeutic group. This is not to say that it had no therapeutic effect on its members, because it had. If anyone should volunteer to link up experiences in his groups or in this very seminar with his own private life he was allowed to do so, but he was not encouraged to do this and sometimes it had to be discouraged. The tradition that evolved was that the reporting registrar was reporting to me as well as to his colleagues at the same time. His colleagues in turn participated freely and frankly, not only in the technical discussion but including very much the question of personal motivation, what in psychoanalysis is called transference and countertransference reactions. In this way the members of the group had a manifold and multifaceted opportunity to learn. This group became quite used to understanding very well and profoundly the deep connection of each colleague's technique, approach, the atmosphere created by him, his reaction to special topics and to other people, and his own personal characteristics, with the purely technical activity with which he was manifestly concerned. The behaviour in this group, the operating group itself, was taken into account, taking its proper place in the psychodynamic procedure, but it was not unduly encouraged or allowed to become a preoccupation of the group. This one sees often happening in similar groups by way of defence. The salient point of it all was that everything which was *relevant* for the work under discussion was taken up. I wish again to stress that everything fell into the right pattern and perspective as long as the conditions and functional purpose of the group was kept clearly in mind.

Individual registrars were continuously changing and there was no question that the central aim was that each as a person should learn as much as possible in this process. The group could indeed exchange shared problems and behaviour, but it was conducted for the individuals' sake. I myself also learned a great deal in looking again and again at this accumulation of interesting experiences concerning the therapeutic group and its conductor and the problems arising through the entanglement and intertwining of these experiences. I believe that this type and method of teaching is not only useful for the teaching of psychotherapists, but of considerable relevance to all other teaching. I myself have made similar experiences and had already used the same principles at Northfield during World War II when asked to introduce my colleagues into the art of group psychotherapy. My observation is that in general this type of group is treated too much like a therapeutic group which is not always to the good. I think one of the reasons for this is that the teacher (usually a practising group therapist) feels more at home, more familiar, more safe, in his role as a therapist than in that of a teacher.

This short reminder of a method of teaching psychotherapy, including group psychotherapy, was included here in view of the likelihood that in the future we shall increasingly be confronted with the task of training doctors and others needed for psychotherapy in a reasonable time though they cannot undergo the full course of training of the expert.

In our present context this example should show two points which seem to me to be significant. First, that this method, the best which is known to me so far for this purpose, seems to fulfil the task we set ourselves; namely to treat and teach psychotherapists in action, in the actual function which they are called upon to perform and in a situation in which problems can be made the subject of study and demonstration. The second point is to show once again the importance of delineating each group situation accurately according to group-analytic principles, and in this way to be clear about its boundaries, about how far it can and should go and where it should not go.

This book therefore ends as it began in showing that the principles which govern our activities in group-analytic psychotherapy operate mutatis mutandis in a great variety of important situations and other tasks in life itself.

References

Abercrombie, M.L.J. *The Anatomy of Judgment*. London, Penguin Books, 1969.

Foulkes, S. H. *Introduction to Group-Analytic Psychotherapy*. London, Heinemann Medical Books, 1948.
Therapeutic Group Analysis. London, Allen & Unwin, 1964.

Foulkes, S.H. and E.J. Anthony. *Group Psychotherapy: The Psychoanalytic Approach*. London, Penguin Books, 1957; revised 1965 and 1973.

Foulkes, S.H. and G.S. Prince (Eds). *Psychiatry in a Changing Society*. London, Tavistock, 1969.

Freud, S. *The Interpretation of Dreams*. Standard Edition, Vols 4 & 5.

Grotjahn, M. *The Voice of the Symbol*. Los Angeles, Mara Books, 1971.

Heigl-Evers, A. and F. Heigl. Indication for Combined Individual and Group Psychotherapy. *Group Analysis*, III/3, 1970.

Miller de Paiva, L. Group Therapy and Psychiatric Rear Guard Action. *Group Analysis*, IV/2, 1971.

Preuss, H.G. Marital Group Therapy. *Group Analysis* IV/2, 1971.

Thompson, S. and J.H. Kahn. *The Group Process as a Helping Technique*. Oxford, Pergamon, 1970.

Index